GRADE 4

Mindset Mathematics

Visualizing and Investigating Big Ideas

Jo Boaler

Jen Munson

Cathy Williams

JOSSEY-BASS™

A Wiley Brand

Published by Jossey-Bass
A Wiley Brand
One Montgomery Street, Suite 1000, San Francisco, CA 94104-4594—www.josseybass.com

Jossey-Bass books and products are available through most bookstores. To contact Jossey-Bass directly call our Customer Care Department within the U.S. at 800-956-7739, outside the U.S. at 317-572-3986, or fax 317-572-4002.

Wiley publishes in a variety of print and electronic formats and by print-on-demand. Some material included with standard print versions of this book may not be included in e-books or in print-on-demand. If this book refers to media such as a CD or DVD that is not included in the version you purchased, you may download this material at http://booksupport.wiley.com. For more information about Wiley products, visit www.wiley.com.

The Visualize, Play, and Investigate icons are used under license from Shutterstock.com and the following arists: Blan-k, Marish, and SuzanaM.

Library of Congress Cataloging-in-Publication Data

Names: Boaler, Jo, 1964- | Munson, Jen, 1977- | Williams, Cathy, 1962-
Title: Mindset mathematics : visualizing and investigating big ideas, grade 4
  / Jo Boaler, Jen Munson, Cathy Williams.
Description: San Francisco, CA : Jossey-Bass, [2017] | Includes index.
Identifiers: LCCN 2017020644 (print) | LCCN 2017022913 (ebook) | ISBN
  9781119358824 (pdf) | ISBN 9781119358817 (epub) | ISBN 9781119358800 (pbk.)
Subjects: LCSH: Games in mathematics education. | Mathematics--Study and
  teaching (Elementary)--Activity programs. | Fourth grade (Education)
Classification: LCC QA20.G35 (ebook) | LCC QA20.G35 B63 2017 (print) | DDC
  372.7/044--dc23
LC record available at https://lccn.loc.gov/2017020644

Cover design by Wiley
Cover image: ©Marish/Shutterstock-Eye; ©Kritchanut/iStockphoto-Background
Printed in the United States of America
FIRST EDITION

V10010496_052619

Contents

Appendix

To all those teachers pursuing a mathematical mindset journey with us.

Introduction

I still remember the moment when Youcubed, the Stanford center I direct, was conceived. I was at the Denver NCSM and NCTM conferences in 2013, and I had arranged to meet Cathy Williams, the director of mathematics for Vista Unified School District. Cathy and I had been working together for the past year improving mathematics teaching in her district. We had witnessed amazing changes taking place, and a filmmaker had documented some of the work. I had recently released my online teacher course, called How to Learn Math, and been overwhelmed by requests from tens of thousands of teachers to provide them with more of the same ideas. Cathy and I decided to create a website and use it to continue sharing the ideas we had used in her district and that I had shared in my online class. Soon after we started sharing ideas on the Youcubed website, we were invited to become a Stanford University center, and Cathy became the codirector of the center with me.

In the months that followed, with the help of one of my undergraduates, Montse Cordero, our first version of youcubed.org was launched. By January 2015, we had managed to raise some money and hire engineers, and we launched a revised version of the site that is close to the site you may know today. We were very excited that in the first month of that relaunch, we had five thousand visits to the site. At the time of writing this, we are now getting three million visits to the site each month. Teachers are excited to learn about the new research and to take the tools, videos, and activities that translate research ideas into practice and use them in their teaching.

Low-Floor, High-Ceiling Tasks

One of the most popular articles on our website is called "Fluency without Fear." I wrote this with Cathy when I heard from many teachers that they were being made to use timed tests in the elementary grades. At the same time, new brain science was emerging showing that when people feel stressed—as students do when facing a timed test—part of their brain, the working memory, is restricted. The working memory is exactly the area of the brain that comes into play when students need to calculate with math facts, and this is the exact area that is impeded when students are stressed. We have evidence now that suggests strongly that timed math tests in the early grades are responsible for the early onset of math anxiety for many students. I teach an undergraduate class at Stanford, and many of the undergraduates are math traumatized. When I ask them what happened to cause this, almost all of them will recall, with startling clarity, the time in elementary school when they were given timed tests. We are really pleased that "Fluency without Fear" has now been used across the United States to pull timed tests out of school districts. It has been downloaded many thousands of times and used in state and national hearings.

One of the reasons for the amazing success of the paper is that it does not just share the brain science on the damage of timed tests but also offers an alternative to timed tests: activities that teach math facts conceptually and through activities that students and teachers enjoy. One of the activities—a game called How Close to 100—became so popular that thousands of teachers tweeted photos of their students playing the game. There was so much attention on Twitter and other media that Stanford noticed and decided to write a news story on the damage of speed to mathematics learning. This was picked up by news outlets across the United States, including *US News & World Report,* which is part of the reason the white paper has now had so many downloads and so much impact. Teachers themselves caused this mini revolution by spreading news of the activities and research.

How Close to 100 is just one of many tasks we have on youcubed.org that are extremely popular with teachers and students. All our tasks have the feature of being "low floor and high ceiling," which I consider to be an extremely important quality for engaging all students in a class. If you are teaching only one student, then a mathematics task can be fairly narrow in terms of its content and difficulty. But whenever you have a group of students, there will be differences in their needs, and they will be challenged by different ideas. A low-floor, high-ceiling task is one in which everyone can engage, no matter what his or her prior understanding or knowledge, but also one that is open enough to extend to high levels, so that all students can be deeply challenged. In the last two years, we have launched an introductory week of mathematics lessons on our site that are open, visual, and low floor, high ceiling. These have been extremely popular with teachers; they have had approximately four million downloads and are used in 20% of schools across the United States.

In our extensive work with teachers around the United States, we are continually asked for more tasks that are like those on our website. Most textbook publishers seem to ignore or be unaware of research on mathematics learning, and most textbook questions are narrow and insufficiently engaging for students. It is imperative that the new knowledge of the ways our brains learn mathematics is incorporated into the lessons students are given in classrooms. It is for this reason that we chose to write a series of books that are organized around a principle of active student engagement, that reflect the latest brain science on learning, and that include activities that are low floor and high ceiling.

Youcubed Summer Camp

We recently brought 81 students onto the Stanford campus for a Youcubed summer math camp, to teach them in the ways that are encouraged in this book. We used open, creative, and visual math tasks. After only 18 lessons with us, the students improved their test score performance by an average of 50%, the equivalent of 1.6 years of school. More important, they changed their relationship with mathematics and started believing in their own potential. They did this, in part, because we talked to them about the brain science showing that

- There is no such thing as a math person—anyone can learn mathematics to high levels.
- Mistakes, struggle, and challenge are critical for brain growth.
- Speed is unimportant in mathematics.
- Mathematics is a visual and beautiful subject, and our brains want to think visually about mathematics.

All of these messages were key to the students' changed mathematics relationship, but just as critical were the tasks we worked on in class. The tasks and the messages about the brain were perfect complements to each other, as we told students they could learn anything, and we showed them a mathematics that was open, creative, and engaging. This approach helped them see that they could learn mathematics and actually do so. This book shares the kinds of tasks that we used in our summer camp, that make up our week of inspirational mathematics (WIM) lessons, and that we post on our site.

Before I outline and introduce the different sections of the book and the ways we are choosing to engage students, I will share some important ideas about how students learn mathematics.

Memorization versus Conceptual Engagement

Many students get the wrong idea about mathematics—exactly the wrong idea. Through years of mathematics classes, many students come to believe that their role in mathematics learning is to memorize methods and facts, and that mathematics success comes from memorization. I say this is exactly the wrong idea because there is actually very little to remember in mathematics. The subject is made up of a few big, linked ideas, and students who are successful in mathematics are those who see the subject as a set of ideas that they need to think deeply about. The Program for International Student Assessment (PISA) tests are international assessments of mathematics, reading, and science that are given every three years. In 2012, PISA not only assessed mathematics achievement but also collected data on students' approach to mathematics. I worked with the PISA team in Paris at the Organisation for Economic Co-operation and Development (OECD) to analyze students' mathematics approaches and their relationship to achievement. One clear result emerged from this analysis. Students approached mathematics in three distinct ways. One group approached mathematics by attempting to memorize the methods they had met; another group took a "relational" approach, relating new concepts to those they already knew; and a third group took a self-monitoring approach, thinking about what they knew and needed to know.

In every country, the memorizers were the lowest-achieving students, and countries with high numbers of memorizers were all lower achieving. In no country were memorizers in the highest-achieving group, and in some high-achieving countries such as Japan, students who combined self-monitoring and relational strategies outscored memorizing students by more than a year's worth of schooling. More detail on this finding is given in this *Scientific American* Mind article that I coauthored with a PISA analyst: https://www.scientificamerican.com/article/why-math-education-in-the-u-s-doesn-t-add-up/.

Mathematics is a conceptual subject, and it is important for students to be thinking slowly, deeply, and conceptually about mathematical ideas, not racing through methods that they try to memorize. One reason that students need to think conceptually has to do with the ways the brain processes mathematics. When we learn new mathematical ideas, they take up a large space in our brain as the brain works out where they fit and what they connect with. But with time, as we move on with our understanding, the knowledge becomes compressed in the brain, taking up a very small space. For first graders, the idea of addition takes up a large space in their brains as they think about how it works and what it means, but for adults the idea of addition is compressed, and it takes up a small space. When adults are asked to add 2 and 3, for example, they can quickly and easily extract the compressed knowledge. William Thurston (1990), a mathematician who won the Field's Medal—the highest honor in mathematics—explains compression like this:

> Mathematics is amazingly compressible: you may struggle a long time, step by step, to work through the same process or idea from several approaches. But once you really understand it and have the mental perspective to see it as a whole, there is often a tremendous mental compression. You can file it away, recall it quickly and completely when you need it, and use it as just one step in some other mental process. The insight that goes with this compression is one of the real joys of mathematics.

You will probably agree with me that not many students think of mathematics as a "real joy," and part of the reason is that they are not compressing mathematical ideas in their brain. This is because the brain only compresses concepts, not methods. So if students are thinking that mathematics is a set of methods to memorize, they are on the wrong pathway, and it is critical that we change that. It is very important that students think deeply and conceptually about ideas. We provide the activities in this book that will allow students to think deeply and conceptually, and an essential role of the teacher is to give the students time to do so.

Mathematical Thinking, Reasoning, and Convincing

When we worked with our Youcubed camp students, we gave each of them journals to record their mathematical thinking. I am a big fan of journaling—for myself and my students. For mathematics students, it helps show them that mathematics is a subject for which we should record ideas and pictures. We can use journaling to encourage students to keep organized records, which is another important part of mathematics, and help them understand that mathematical thinking can be a long and slow process. Journals also give students free space—where they can be creative, share ideas, and feel ownership of their work. We did not write in the students' journals, as we wanted them to think of the journals as their space, not something that teachers wrote on. We gave students feedback on sticky notes that we stuck onto their work. The images in Figure I.1 show some of the mathematical records the camp students kept in their journals.

Another resource I always share with learners is the act of color coding—that is, students using colors to highlight different ideas. For example, when working on an algebraic task, they may show the *x* in the same color in an expression, in a graph, and in a picture, as shown in Figure I.2.

When adding numbers, color coding may help show the addends (Figure I.3).

Color coding highlights connections, which are a really critical part of mathematics.

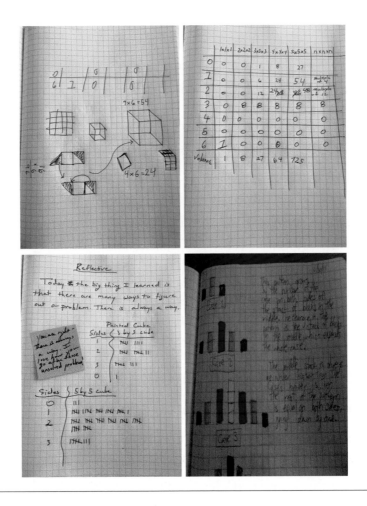

Figure I.1

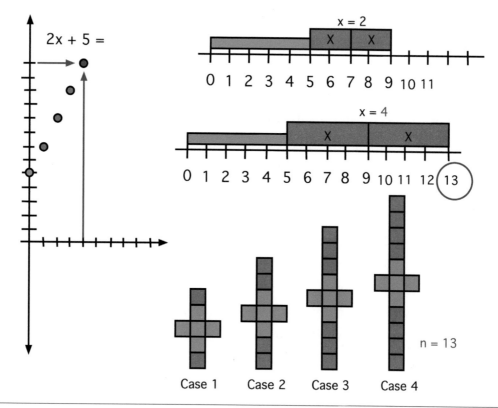

Figure I.2

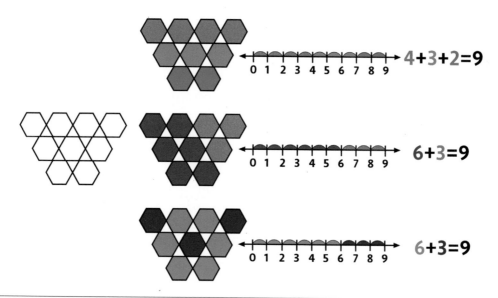

Figure I.3

Another important part of mathematics is the act of reasoning—explaining why methods are chosen and how steps are linked, and using logic to connect ideas. Reasoning is at the heart of mathematics. Scientists prove ideas by finding more cases that fit a theory, or countercases that contradict a theory, but mathematicians prove their work by reasoning. If students are not reasoning, then they are not really doing mathematics. In the activities of these books, we suggest a framework that encourages students to be convincing when they reason. We tell them that there are three levels of being convincing. The first, or easiest, level is to convince yourself of something. A higher level is to convince a friend. And the highest level of all is to convince a skeptic. We also share with students that they should be skeptics with one another, asking one another why methods were chosen and how they work. We have found this framework to be very powerful with students; they enjoy being skeptics, pushing each other to deeper levels of reasoning, and it encourages students to reason clearly, which is important for their learning.

We start each book in our series with an activity that invites students to reason about mathematics and be convincing. I first met an activity like this when reading Mark Driscoll's teaching ideas in his book *Fostering Algebraic Thinking*. I thought it was a perfect activity for introducing the skeptics framework that I had learned from a wonderful teacher, Cathy Humphreys. She had learned about and adapted the framework from two of my inspirational teachers from England: mathematician John Mason and mathematics educator Leone Burton. As well as encouraging students to be convincing, in a number of activities we ask students to prove an idea. Some people think of proof as a formal set of steps that they learned in geometry class. But the act of proving is really about connecting ideas, and as students enter the learning journey of proving, it is worthwhile celebrating their steps toward formal proof. Mathematician Paul Lockhart (2012) rejects the idea that proving is about following a set of formal steps, instead proposing that proving is "abstract art, pure and simple. And art is always a struggle. There is no systematic way of creating beautiful and meaningful paintings or sculptures, and there is also no method for producing beautiful and meaningful mathematical arguments" (p. 8). Instead of suggesting that students follow formal steps, we invite them to think deeply about mathematical concepts and make connections. Students will be given many ways to be creative when they prove and justify, and for reasons I discuss later, we always encourage and celebrate visual as well as numerical and algebraic justifications. Ideally, students will create visual, numerical, and algebraic representations and connect their ideas through color coding and through verbal explanations. Students are excited to experience mathematics in these ways, and they benefit from the opportunity to bring their individual ideas and creativity to the problem-solving and learning space. As students develop in their mathematical understanding, we can encourage them to extend and generalize their ideas through reasoning, justifying, and proving. This process deepens their understanding and helps them compress their learning.

Big Ideas

The books in the Mindset Mathematics Series are all organized around mathematical "big ideas." Mathematics is not a set of methods; it is a set of connected ideas that need to be understood. When students understand the big ideas in mathematics, the methods and rules fall into place. One of the reasons any set of curriculum standards is flawed is that standards take the beautiful subject of mathematics and its many connections, and divide it into small pieces that make the connections disappear. Instead of starting with the small pieces, we have started with the big ideas and important connections, and have listed the relevant Common Core curriculum standards within the activities. Our activities invite students to engage in the mathematical acts that are listed in the imperative Common Core practice standards, and they also teach many of the Common Core content standards, which emerge from the rich activities.

Although we have chapters for each big idea, as though they are separate from each other, they are all intrinsically linked. Figure I.4 shows some of the connections between the ideas, and you may be able to see others. It is very important to share with students that mathematics is a subject of connections and to highlight the connections as students work. You may want to print the color visual of the different connections for students to see as they work.

Structure of the Book

Visualize. Play. Investigate. These three words provide the structure for each book in the series. They also pave the way for open student thinking, for powerful brain

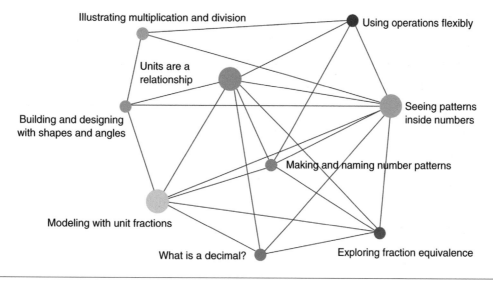

Figure I.4

connections, for engagement, and for deep understanding. How do they do that? And why is this book so different from other mathematics curriculum books?

Visualize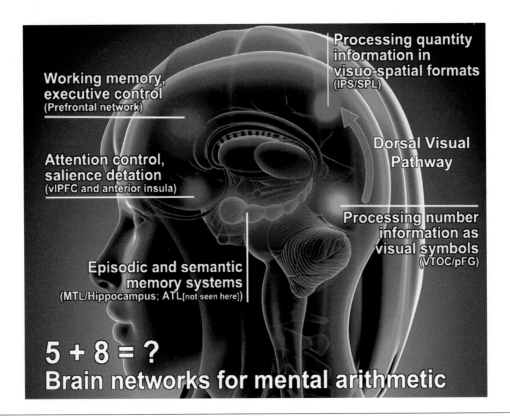

For the past few years, I have been working with a neuroscience group at Stanford, under the direction of Vinod Menon, which specializes in mathematics learning. We have been working together to think about the ways that findings from brain science can be used to help learners of mathematics. One of the exciting discoveries that has been emerging over the last few years is the importance of visualizing for the brain and our learning of mathematics. Brain scientists now know that when we work on mathematics, even when we perform a bare number calculation, five areas of the brain are involved, as shown in Figure I.5.

Two of the five brain pathways—the dorsal and ventral pathways—are visual. The dorsal visual pathway is the main brain region for representing quantity. This may seem surprising, as so many of us have sat through hundreds of hours of mathematics classes working with numbers, while barely ever engaging visually with mathematics. Now brain scientists know that our brains "see" fingers when we calculate,

Figure I.5

and knowing fingers well—what they call finger perception—is critical for the development of an understanding of number. If you would like to read more about the importance of finger work in mathematics, look at the visual mathematics section of youcubed.org. Number lines are really helpful, as they provide the brain with a visual representation of number order. In one study, a mere four 15-minute sessions of students playing with a number line completely eradicated the differences between students from low-income and middle-income backgrounds coming into school (Siegler & Ramani, 2008).

Our brain wants to think visually about mathematics, yet few curriculum materials engage students in visual thinking. Some mathematics books show pictures, but they rarely ever invite students to do their own visualizing and drawing. The neuroscientists' research shows the importance not only of visual thinking but also of students' connecting different areas of their brains as they work on mathematics. The scientists now know that as children learn and develop, they increase the connections between different parts of the brain, and they particularly develop connections between symbolic and visual representations of numbers. Increased mathematics achievement comes about when students are developing those connections. For so long, our emphasis in mathematics education has been on symbolic representations of numbers, with students developing one area of the brain that is concerned with symbolic number representation. A more productive and engaging approach is to develop all areas of the brain that are involved in mathematical thinking, and visual connections are critical to this development.

In addition to the brain development that occurs when students think visually, we have found that visual activities are really engaging for students. Even students who think they are "not visual learners" (an incorrect idea) become fascinated and think deeply about mathematics that is shown visually—such as the visual representations of the calculation 18 × 5 shown in Figure I.6.

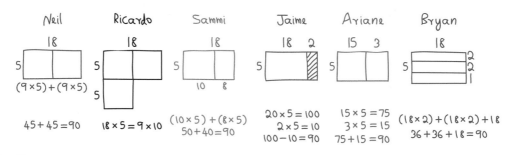

Figure I.6

In our Youcubed teaching of summer school to sixth- and seventh-grade students and in our trialing of Youcubed's WIM materials, we have found that students are inspired by the creativity that is possible when mathematics is visual. When we were trialing the materials in a local middle school one day, a parent stopped me and asked what we had been doing. She said that her daughter had always said she hated and couldn't do math, but after working on our tasks, she came home saying she could see a future for herself in mathematics. We had been working on the number visuals that we use throughout these teaching materials, shown in Figure I.7.

The parent reported that when her daughter had seen the creativity possible in mathematics, everything had changed for her. I strongly believe that we can give these insights and inspirations to many more learners with the sort of creative, open mathematics tasks that fill this book.

We have also found that when we present visual activities to students, the status differences that often get in the way of good mathematics teaching disappear. I was visiting a first-grade classroom recently, and the teacher had set up four different stations around the room. In all of them, the students were working on arithmetic. In one, the teacher engaged students in a mini number talk; in another, a teaching

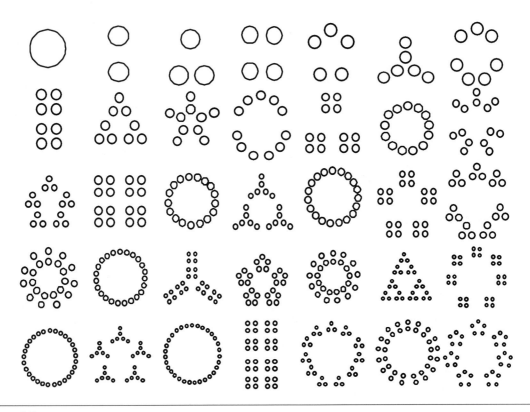

Figure I.7

assistant worked on an activity with coins; in the third, the students played a board game; and in the fourth, they worked on a number worksheet. In each of the first three stations, the students collaborated and worked really well, but as soon as students went to the worksheet station, conversations changed, and in every group I heard statements like "This is easy," " I've finished," "I can't do this," and "Haven't you finished yet?" These status comments are unfortunate and off-putting for many students. I now try to present mathematical tasks without numbers as often as possible, or I take out the calculation part of a task, as it is the numerical and calculational aspects that often cause students to feel less sure of themselves. This doesn't mean that students cannot have a wonderful and productive relationship with numbers, as we hope to promote in this book, but sometimes the key mathematical idea can be arrived at without any numbers at all.

Almost all the tasks in our book invite students to think visually about mathematics and to connect visual and numerical representations. This encourages important brain connections as well as deep student engagement.

Play

The key to reducing status differences in mathematics classrooms, in my view, comes from *opening* mathematics. When we teach students that we can see or approach any mathematical idea in different ways, they start to respect the different thinking of all students. Opening mathematics involves inviting students to see ideas differently, explore with ideas, and ask their own questions. Students can gain access to the same mathematical ideas and methods through creativity and exploration that they can by being taught methods that they practice. As well as reducing or removing status differences, open mathematics is more engaging for students. This is why we are inviting students, through these mathematics materials, to play with mathematics. Albert Einstein famously once said that "play is the highest form of research." This is because play is an opportunity for ideas to be used and developed in the service of something enjoyable. In the Play activities of our materials, students are invited to work with an important idea in a free space where they can enjoy the freedom of mathematical play. This does not mean that the activities do not teach essential mathematical content and practices—they do, as they invite students to work with the ideas. We have designed the Play activities to downplay competition and instead invite students to work with each other, building understanding together.

Investigate ❓

Our Investigate activities add something very important: they give students opportunities to take ideas to the sky. They also have a playful element, but the difference is that they pose questions that students can explore and take to very high levels. As I mentioned earlier, all of our tasks are designed to be as low floor and high ceiling as possible, as these provide the best conditions for engaging all students, whatever their prior knowledge. Any student can access them, and students can take the ideas to high levels. We should always be open to being surprised by what our learners can do, and always provide all students with opportunities to take work to high levels and to be challenged.

A crucial finding from neuroscience is the importance of students struggling and making mistakes—these are the times when brains grow the most. In one of my meetings with a leading neuroscientist, he stated it very clearly: if students are not struggling, they are not learning. We want to put students into situations where they feel that work is hard, but within their reach. Do not worry if students ask questions that you don't know the answer to; that is a good thing. One of the damaging ideas that teachers and students share in education is that teachers of mathematics know everything. This gives students the idea that mathematics people are those who know a lot and never make mistakes, which is an incorrect and harmful message. It is good to say to your students, "That is a great question that we can all think about" or "I have never thought about that idea; let's investigate it together." It is even good to make mistakes in front of students, as it shows them that mistakes are an important part of mathematical work. As they investigate, they should be going to places you have never thought about—taking ideas in new directions and exploring uncharted territory. Model for students what it means to be a curious mathematics learner, always open to learning new ideas and being challenged yourself.

*   *   *

We have designed activities to take at least a class period, but some of them could go longer, especially if students ask deep questions or start an investigation into a cool idea. If you can be flexible about students' time on activities, that is ideal, or you may wish to suggest that students continue activities at home. In our teaching of these activities, we have found that students are so excited by the ideas that they take them home to their families and continue working on them, which is wonderful. At all times, celebrate deep thinking over speed, as that is the nature of real mathematical thought. Ask students to come up with creative representations of their ideas; celebrate their drawing, modeling, and any form of creativity. Invite your students into a journey of mathematical curiosity and take that journey with them, walking by their side as they experience the wonder of open, mindset mathematics.

References

Lockhart, P. (2012). *Measurement.* Cambridge, MA: Harvard University Press.

Siegler, R. S., & Ramani, G. B. (2008). Playing linear numerical board games promotes low income children's numerical development. *Developmental Science, 11*(5), 655–661. doi:10.1111/j.1467-7687.2008.00714.x

Thurston, W. (1990). Mathematical education. *Notices of the American Mathematical Society, 37*(7), 844–850.

Activities for Building Norms

Encouraging Good Group Work

We always use this activity before students work on math together, as it helps improve group interactions. Teachers who have tried this activity have been pleased by students' thoughtful responses and found the students' thoughts and words helpful in creating a positive and supportive environment. The first thing to do is to ask students, in groups, to reflect on things they don't like people to say or do in a group when they are working on math together. Students come up with quite a few important ideas, such as not liking people to give away the answer, to rush through the work, or to ignore other people's ideas. When students have had enough time in groups brainstorming, collect the ideas. We usually do this by making a What We Don't Like list or poster and asking each group to contribute one idea, moving around the room until a few good ideas have been shared (usually about 10). Then we do the same for the What We Do Like list or poster. It can be good to present the final posters to the class as the agreed-on classroom norms that you and they can reflect back on over the year. If any student shares a negative comment, such as "I don't like waiting for slow people," do not put it on the poster; instead use it as a chance to discuss the issue. This rarely happens, and students are usually very thoughtful and respectful in the ideas they share.

Activity	Time	Description/Prompt	Materials
Launch	5 min	Explain to students that working in groups is an important part of what mathematicians do. Mathematicians discuss their ideas and work together to solve challenging problems. It's important to work together, and we need to discuss what helps us work well together.	
Explore	10 min	Assign a group facilitator to make sure that all students get to share their thoughts on points 1 and 2. Groups should record every group member's ideas and then decide which they will share during the whole-class discussion. In your groups . . . 1. Reflect on the things you do not like people to say or do when you are working on math together in a group. 2. Reflect on the things you do like people to say or do when you are working on math together in a group.	• Paper • Pencil or pen
Discuss	10 min	Ask each group to share their findings. Condense their responses and make a poster so that the student ideas are visible and you can refer to them during the class.	Two to four pieces of large poster paper to collect the students' ideas

Paper Folding: Learning to Reason, Convince, and Be Skeptical

> Connection to CCSS
> 4.G.2

One of the most important topics in mathematics is reasoning. Whereas scientists prove or disprove ideas by finding cases, mathematicians prove their ideas by reasoning—making logical connections between ideas. This activity gives students an opportunity to learn to reason well by having to convince others who are being skeptical.

Before beginning the activity, explain to students that their role is to be convincing. The easiest person to convince is yourself. A higher level of being convincing is to convince a friend, and the highest level of all is to convince a skeptic. In this activity, the students learn to reason to the extent that they can convince a skeptic. Students should work in pairs and take it in turns to be the one convincing and the one being a skeptic.

Give each student a square piece of paper. If you already have 8.5 × 11 paper, you can ask them to make the square first.

The first challenge is for one of the students to fold the paper to make a triangle that does not include any of the edges of the paper. She should convince her partner that it is a triangle, using what she knows about triangles to be convincing. The skeptic partner should ask lots of skeptical questions, such as "How do you know that it is a 90-degree angle?" and not accept that it is because it looks like one.

The partners should then switch roles, and the other student folds the paper into a square that does not include any of the edges of the paper. His partner should be skeptical and push for high levels of reasoning.

The partners should then switch again, and the challenge is to fold the paper to make an isosceles triangle, again not using the edges of the paper.

The fourth challenge is to make a different isosceles triangle. For each challenge, partners must reason and be skeptical.

When the task is complete, facilitate a whole-class discussion in which students discuss the following questions:

- Which was the most challenging task? Why?
- What was hard about reasoning and being convincing?
- What was hard about being a skeptic?

Activity	Time	Description/Prompt	Materials
Launch	5 min	Tell students that their role for the day is to be convincing and to be a skeptic. Ask students to fold a piece of paper into a right scalene triangle. Choose a student and model being a skeptic.	
Explore	10 min	Show students the task and explain that in each round, they are to solve the folding problem. In pairs, students alternate folding and reasoning and being the skeptic. After students convince themselves they have solved each problem, they switch roles and fold the next challenge. Give students square paper or ask them to start by making a square. The convincing challenges are as follows: 1. Fold your paper into a triangle that does not include any edges of the paper. 2. Fold your paper into a square that does not include any edges of the paper. 3. Fold your paper into an isosceles triangle that does not include any edges of the paper. 4. Fold your paper into a different isosceles triangle that does not include any edges of the paper.	• One piece of 8.5" × 11" paper per student • Paper Folding worksheet for each student
Discuss	10 min	Discuss the activity as a class. Make sure to discuss the roles of convincer and skeptic.	

Paper Folding: Learning to Reason, Convince, and Be a Skeptic

1. Fold your paper into a triangle that does not include any edges of the paper. Convince a skeptic that it is a triangle.

   Reflection:

   Switch roles

2. Fold your paper into a square that does not include any edges of the paper. Convince a skeptic that it is a square.

   Reflection:

   Switch roles

3. Fold your paper into an isosceles triangle that does not include any edges of the paper. Convince a skeptic that it is an isosceles triangle.

   Reflection:

   Switch roles

4. Fold your paper into a different isosceles triangle that does not include any edges of the paper. Convince a skeptic that it is an isosceles triangle.

   Reflection:

BIG IDEA **1**

Seeing Patterns inside Numbers

Numbers make up our world, and they are used throughout our lives, whatever our age, job, or level of interest. But many people develop a narrow relationship with numbers, seeing them as something to use in calculations, rather than as a fascinating set of ideas that can enrich their world. Our first big idea invites students to become captivated by numbers and to get to know numbers deeply. What is enchanting about numbers is that they are all made up of different arrangements, have different factors, can be seen differently, and have their own intricate system to be explored.

When we first came across Brent Vorgey's number visual (Figure 1.1), we were enthralled, as we immediately saw the creativity, beauty, and insights that the visual representations revealed.

In our Visualize activity, we invite students to explore this depiction of numbers and to see what patterns are uncovered by the visual representations. We invite them to see what primes look like and to see the different factors inside numbers. We invite them to investigate patterns among the numbers, seeing what their positioning on the diagram reveals. Also, we invite students to see numbers visually and to develop a realization that numbers contain all sorts of information that make them different from each other, special, and interesting.

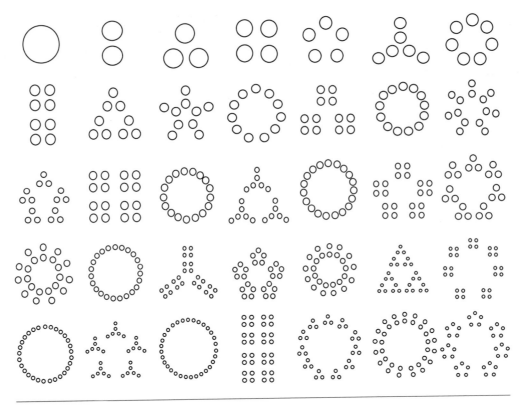

Figure 1.1

In the Play activity, we extend students' time with the number visuals in a more playful setting. Students play a game with the number visual page as a game board, and move between visual and numerical representations. This, as with the other two tasks in this big idea, encourages important connections between different areas of the brain.

In the Investigate activity, we invite students to think carefully about number flexibility. One of the ways that numbers are different from one another is the number of factors they have and the degree of flexibility they give us when using them. For example, 24 is a very flexible number, as it can be broken up in all sorts of different ways. This makes it a useful number for packaging, for designing, and for measuring time. In this activity, we invite students to give value to different numbers according to their flexibility, helping them develop an appreciation for these numbers. The activity also invites students to make equal groups and gives teachers an opportunity to discuss whether students are thinking additively or multiplicatively and what those differences mean.

All three activities give students an opportunity to develop new insights into the numbers that they will use for the rest of their lives.

Brain science tells us that when students are engaging with numbers as symbols, such as the numeral 4, and with numbers as visuals, as shown in Figure 1.2, they are connecting between different areas of the brain, and such connections are critical for mathematics learning and achievement. The activities in this big idea will invite a lot of brain connecting, with students developing pathways that will help them as they go forward in their mathematical careers.

Jo Boaler

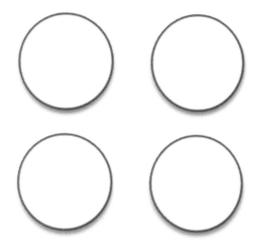

Figure 1.2

Visualizing Numbers

Snapshot

In this activity, students work with the number visual page to explore the patterns that they can see inside of numbers. In this activity, we open the door to understanding factors, multiples, and primes, as well as other number patterns.

Connection to CCSS
4.OA.4

Agenda

Activity	Time	Description/Prompt	Materials
Launch	5 min	Generate multiple ways that numbers can be represented and introduce the number visual page.	Number visual page reproduced for students and one to display
Explore	20+min	Students look for patterns inside the number visual page and color-code them.	Colors for students (colored pencils, markers, or pens)
Discuss	10 min	Discuss the different patterns students found and how their color coding makes the patterns visible.	
Explore	20+min	Student look for patterns shared across the different numbers. Student cut their papers so that they can group or arrange them to show shared patterns.	• Number visual page, one per group • Colors • Scissors • Optional: posters or large paper
Discuss	15 min	Students share the different ways they have grouped the numbers and discuss the shared patterns they have found.	

To the Teacher

The length of this lesson depends largely on how long students would like to explore patterns. We've found that some students want to explore patterns in depth, and they should be given time to do that. Follow your students' lead and interest. This activity can easily be spread across multiple days.

Activity

Launch

Numbers can be represented in lots of different ways. For example, 6 can be written as a numeral, but 6 can also be shown in other ways, as in Figure 1.3.

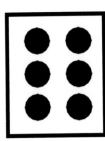

Figure 1.3

When you launch this activity, you may want to share some of these ways with students or have them generate ways that numbers are represented in their world. Give each student a copy of the number visual page and ask them to notice what numbers are shown. Have them record the actual number value by each visual. There are patterns all over this page. Ask students, what patterns do you notice?

Explore

Ask students to investigate the patterns in the number visual page.

- What patterns do you see?

Provide students with colors (colored pencils, pens, or markers).

- How can you use color to show the patterns within these numbers?

Students might notice equal-size groups within some numbers. For instance, 4, 8, 12, 16, 20, 24, 28, and 32 all have square clusters of 4 inside them. Students might notice that some numbers have no groups inside them; numbers like 11, 13, 17, and 19 are circles. Students might notice how some numbers grow outward from a central pattern. For instance, 6 has a group of 3 in the center, and each corner has been added onto with one dot. Students might also notice multiple numbers inside one number. For instance, 18 has three groups of 6, but also has 9 pairs. Some of these patterns are shown in Figure 1.4 as an example of how students might use color to highlight different patterns they see.

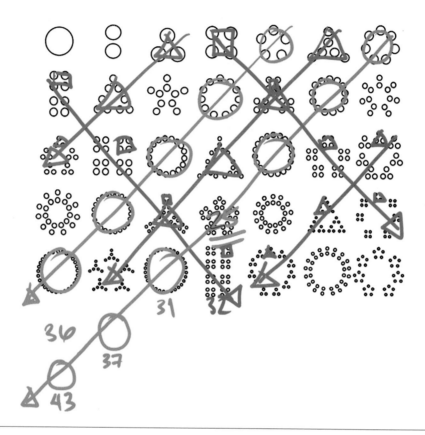

Figure 1.4

Discuss

Ask students to share the different ways they have color-coded their numbers to reveal patterns. What do different ways of coloring show? You may want to focus discussion on a single number to compare the different patterns inside. For instance, you could look at the different patterns inside of 12 that different ways of coloring make clear.

What do different numbers have in common? If you focused on a particular number, you might ask, What other numbers are like this number? How are they alike? If students notice the clusters within each number, give them the term *factor* to describe these clusters. For instance, if students see the three clusters of 4 inside 12, you can say that 4 is a factor of 12, or that 12 has 4 as a factor.

Explore

Now ask students to return to their color-coded number visuals and look for patterns that different numbers share. Provide students with a new number visual page and scissors to cut this new page apart so that they can group, sort, or web numbers by common features and color-code those features. Students should work with a partner or in a small group to find patterns.

- What patterns do different numbers share?
- How can you group or arrange the numbers to show what numbers have in common?

You might have students glue or tape their arrangements onto a poster to make sharing easier. This way, they could label the groups or the relationships between the numbers.

Discuss

Ask students to share the patterns they notice between numbers. You may want to have students hang their posters and do a gallery walk, or ask each group to share what they have found. In either case, discuss as a class the following questions:

- What patterns do different numbers share?
- What are you wondering now about these numbers?
- What are you wondering about the numbers we haven't looked at yet?

If students notice the clusters that different number share, be sure to tell them that we say that they share a factor. If students notice the circles and the lack of clusters within, be sure to probe what this means. You can name these numbers, where no equal groups are possible, as *prime*.

Look-Fors

- **Do students notice that numbers are inside of other numbers?** For instance, does anyone see three clusters of 4 inside of 12? One goal of this activity is for students to see the building blocks of numbers.
- **Do students notice that some numbers are made only of individual dots?** This is the beginning of noticing primes.

- **Are students thinking multiplicatively or additively?** Although numbers can be broken apart through addition, we want to push students to notice patterns of equal groups. This is an interesting point of discussion.
- **Are students noticing that some numbers have similar building blocks?** This is the beginning of noticing common factors.

Reflect

What do you think is the most interesting number on this page? Why?

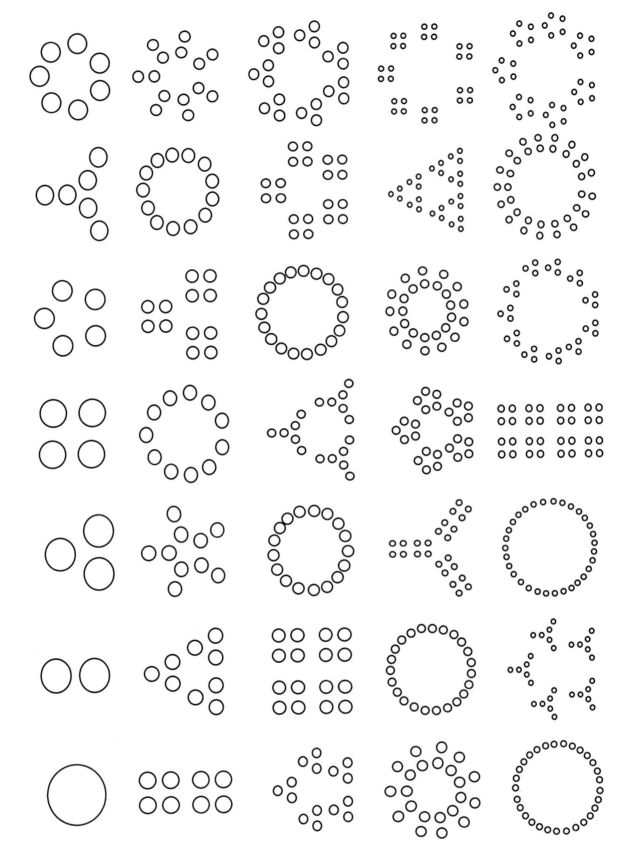

Mindset Mathematics, Grade 4, copyright © 2017 by Jo Boaler, Jen Munson, Cathy Williams.
Reproduced by permission of John Wiley & Sons, Inc.

What Could It Be?

Snapshot

Students play a game using the number visuals to further explore the idea of factors. Pairs of students each try to claim four squares in a row on a number game board, while thinking both visually and numerically.

Connection to CCSS
4.OA.4

Agenda

Activity	Time	Description/Prompt	Materials
Launch	10 min	Introduce the idea of a number part and teach students the rules of today's game.	• Visual Number Part Cards (one deck per partnership) • Game boards (at least one per partnership) • Marking tools: pencils, colors, or chips
Play	20+ min	Students play What Could It Be? in partnerships.	
Discuss	10 min	Discuss the strategies students developed playing the game.	

To the Teacher

Today's game uses the number visuals students explored in the Visualize activity. Different game boards are provided that pose different degrees of challenge; the board with larger numbers and the board where the values are not in order are more challenging. Students will play in pairs, and may play with one board initially and then want to try a more challenging board.

Activity

Launch

Display one of the Visual Number Part Cards or zoom in on one of the visual numbers so that only a portion is visible to students. Tell students that this is just a part of a larger number. Ask the class, What number could this be? You may want to ask student to partner to share ideas and reasoning. Collect from the class some possible answers and the reasoning that supports them. You might also want to ask, What number could it not be? Why not?

Introduce today's game by showing students a game board. We suggest starting with the 1–36 game board. Without fully playing the game with students, explain the rules, showing students how they could have marked the number visual they just discussed as a class.

Play

Game Directions

- Set up the game space by placing a game board between you and your partner. Put the card deck face down between you. Each player will need a pencil, color, or a set of chips to mark the board.
- Partners take turns drawing a Visual Number Part Card. The player drawing the card must figure out, "What number could it be?" and share their reasoning with their partner. Then the player can mark (with an X, color, or chip) the number they chose.
- Players take turns drawing, reasoning, and marking numbers until one player marks four squares in a row, horizontally, vertically, or diagonally.

As students play, you'll want to walk around and see what kind of reasoning students are using, what possibilities they come up with, and whether they may want a more challenging board. Students can play repeatedly on the same board. You may decide you want to change partnerships midway through the play time so that students can try their strategies out on someone new.

Discuss

Bring students together to discuss the strategies they developed during the game. Discuss the following questions:

- How did you decide what numbers a picture might represent?
- How did you then choose which of those numbers you would mark?
- What made the game hard? Did you make any mistakes? What did you learn from those mistakes?
- Which numbers were easiest to capture? Which were hardest? Why do you think that is?

Look-Fors

- **How are students reasoning about the numbers each picture could represent? Are they applying thinking about factors?** The portions on the card should support students in beginning to generate multiples and think about how the factors can be used to build a larger number.
- **Do students recognize which kinds of pictures could be prime numbers?** The primes on the game board are particularly challenging, and students will need to notice that only some cards could be used to capture those numbers.

Reflect

How would you make an easy game board? A very challenging game board?

Visual Number Part Cards

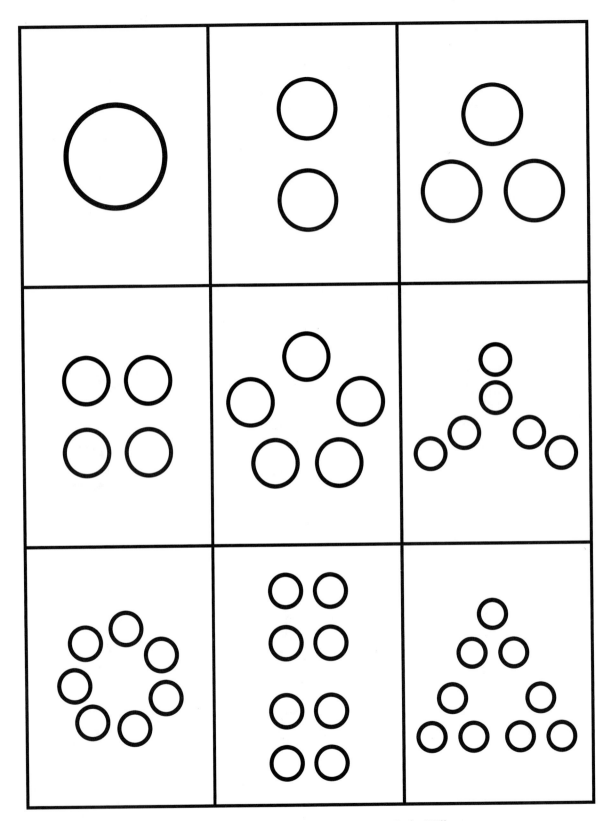

Mindset Mathematics, Grade 4, copyright © 2017 by Jo Boaler, Jen Munson, Cathy Williams.
Reproduced by permission of John Wiley & Sons, Inc.

Visual Number Part Cards

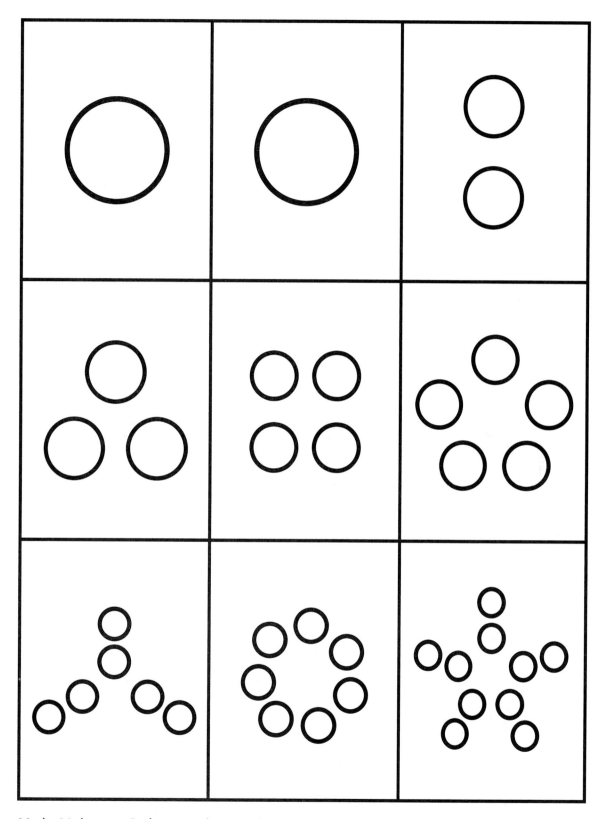

Mindset Mathematics, Grade 4, copyright © 2017 by Jo Boaler, Jen Munson, Cathy Williams.
Reproduced by permission of John Wiley & Sons, Inc.

Game Board 1

1	2	3	4	5	6
7	8	9	10	11	12
13	14	15	16	17	18
19	20	21	22	23	24
25	26	27	28	29	30
31	32	33	34	35	36

1. _____ x _____ = _____

2. _____ x _____ = _____

3. _____ x _____ = _____

4. _____ x _____ = _____

5. _____ x _____ = _____

6. _____ x _____ = _____

7. _____ x _____ = _____

8. _____ x _____ = _____

9. _____ x _____ = _____

10. _____ x _____ = _____

11. _____ x _____ = _____

12. _____ x _____ = _____

13. _____ x _____ = _____

14. _____ x _____ = _____

15. _____ x _____ = _____

Game Board 2

1	2	3	4	5	6	7	8
9	10	11	12	13	14	15	16
17	18	19	20	21	22	23	24
25	26	27	28	29	30	31	32
33	34	35	36	37	38	39	40
41	42	45	46	48	49	50	51
52	54	55	56	60	63	64	65
69	70	72	73	75	77	80	81

1. _____ x _____ = _____

2. _____ x _____ = _____

3. _____ x _____ = _____

4. _____ x _____ = _____

5. _____ x _____ = _____

6. _____ x _____ = _____

7. _____ x _____ = _____

8. _____ x _____ = _____

9. _____ x _____ = _____

10. _____ x _____ = _____

11. _____ x _____ = _____

12. _____ x _____ = _____

13. _____ x _____ = _____

14. _____ x _____ = _____

15. _____ x _____ = _____

16. _____ x _____ = _____

17. _____ x _____ = _____

18. _____ x _____ = _____

19. _____ x _____ = _____

20. _____ x _____ = _____

21. _____ x _____ = _____

22. _____ x _____ = _____

23. _____ x _____ = _____

24. _____ x _____ = _____

Game Board 3

37	3	9	13	27	19	22	48
10	31	39	45	15	81	60	28
17	34	20	21	18	30	23	14
38	72	27	69	29	40	31	32
33	12	1	36	11	26	50	2
41	64	80	16	4	49	55	42
52	75	5	56	7	63	6	65
35	70	18	8	13	77	54	51

1. _____ x _____ = _____

2. _____ x _____ = _____

3. _____ x _____ = _____

4. _____ x _____ = _____

5. _____ x _____ = _____

6. _____ x _____ = _____

7. _____ x _____ = _____

8. _____ x _____ = _____

9. _____ x _____ = _____

10. _____ x _____ = _____

11. _____ x _____ = _____

12. _____ x _____ = _____

13. _____ x _____ = _____

14. _____ x _____ = _____

15. _____ x _____ = _____

16. _____ x _____ = _____

17. _____ x _____ = _____

18. _____ x _____ = _____

19. _____ x _____ = _____

20. _____ x _____ = _____

21. _____ x _____ = _____

22. _____ x _____ = _____

23. _____ x _____ = _____

24. _____ x _____ = _____

How Flexible Is a Number?

Snapshot

In this activity, we extend the work students have been doing with the number visuals and focus on the importance of factors for making numbers useful and flexible. Making equal groups is a central idea for number flexibility and is a different way of decomposing numbers than students may often use.

Connection to CCSS
4.OA.4

Agenda

Activity	Time	Description/Prompt	Materials
Launch	5 min	Ask why some numbers are used frequently in our world and some are not. Set up the investigation of number flexibility.	Optional: items in packages or photos to show
Explore	20+ min	Students work in small groups to determine the relative flexibility of a set of numbers and arrange them in a line.	• Visual Number Part Cards, in small sets for each group • Optional: cubes, tiles, chips, or other manipulatives
Discuss	25+ min	The class works together to construct a shared continuum of flexibility. The discussion closes with developing a definition of flexibility.	• Line on the wall, with ends labeled "Inflexible" and "Most Flexible" • Tape or pushpins for posting numbers
Extend	25+ min	Students investigate a number (36–100) of their choosing and determine where to place it on the continuum.	Additional paper

To the Teacher

In the work students do to solve problems, they often identify meaningful and useful ways to decompose numbers. These ways sometimes use equal groups, such as when students break 18 into two groups of 9. But often students use other ways to decompose, like place value (18 = 10 + 8) or compensation (18 = 20 − 2). In today's activity, the goal is for students to think about equal groups as a useful way to decompose, and to see those equal groups as factors. You might notice some students thinking simply about the additive ways that a number can be decomposed—for instance, that 18 is 17 + 1, 16 + 2, 15 + 3, and so on. This kind of thinking will make it difficult for students to see the flexibility of numbers based on factors. Encourage students to think about the context of the task: Why are some numbers often used in making packages of items while others aren't? You might encourage students to draw pictures of these packages as part of their investigation to help them visualize what makes these numbers useful and flexible. Flexibility can often be seen in the arrangement of the objects in arrays.

Activity

Launch

Launch by telling students that some numbers are used a lot in our world, and some numbers rarely show up. In the grocery store, students might notice that eggs come in a carton of 12, and bottled water is also sold in cases of 12. Pose the questions, Why not 11? or 13? Collect some ideas from students about why this might be.

What makes a number so flexible that it can be used in lots of different ways? What makes a number inflexible? Tell students that they will be working together to investigate these questions. The class will make a display of how flexible or inflexible students think these numbers are, using evidence about each number.

Explore

Students work in groups and receive a set of numbers from the Visual Number Part Cards. Be sure that each group gets a diverse set of numbers, a mix of primes and composites. For instance, a group could get 2, 7, 8, 25, and 29. Make sure each group gets at least one of these numbers: 8, 12, 16, 18, 20, 24, 30.

Students work together to investigate how flexible each number is. You may want to provide tiles, chips, cubes, or additional paper. Students record their evidence of flexibility on the number cards or additional paper.

Then students in each group work to come to consensus about how to rank the flexibility of the numbers in their set. Students then arrange their numbers in a line to show the most flexible on one end and inflexible on the other end. They might decide that some numbers are equally flexible. Whatever their argument, the group should be prepared to justify their findings.

Discuss

Bring the groups together to cocreate a display on the board or one wall of your classroom. Have a horizontal line on your wall with labels at either end for "Inflexible" and "Most Flexible." The goal of this discussion is to create a continuum of number flexibility, building on ideas around factors, multiples, and primes. Students need to convince the class where the numbers their group investigated should go on this continuum. You may want to have each group present in turn, convincing the class where their numbers should go in relationship to the numbers that have already been placed. Students may conclude that some numbers need to be moved. To move a number, students need to convince their classmates where it should be placed. Alternately, you may want to have each group place one number, give their reasoning, and field any questions from the class. Rotate from group to group until all numbers have been presented, explained, and agreed on.

Close the discussion by coming up with a class definition, based on all that you have discussed, of what qualities define "inflexible" and "most flexible. Add these definitions to the labels on your continuum.

Extend

Ask groups to now choose a number between 36 and 100. Have students create a number image for that number, investigate the number's flexibility, and decide as a group where it should be placed on the class continuum. Groups can share these numbers and justify their placement in a second discussion. You could decide to set students a goal of finding a particularly flexible or inflexible number in this extension.

Look-Fors

- **Are students thinking multiplicatively or additively?** The goal of this lesson is to be thinking about making equal groups and the many ways you can break a number into equal groups.

- **Are students focusing on the number of factors a given number has?** This is one criterion for flexibility.

- **Are students noticing that some factors are themselves composites and some are prime?** You may want to probe why this matters in making numbers flexible or not.

Reflect

If you wanted to find an inflexible number, how would you do it? If you wanted to find a very flexible number, how would you do it?

Visual Number Part Cards

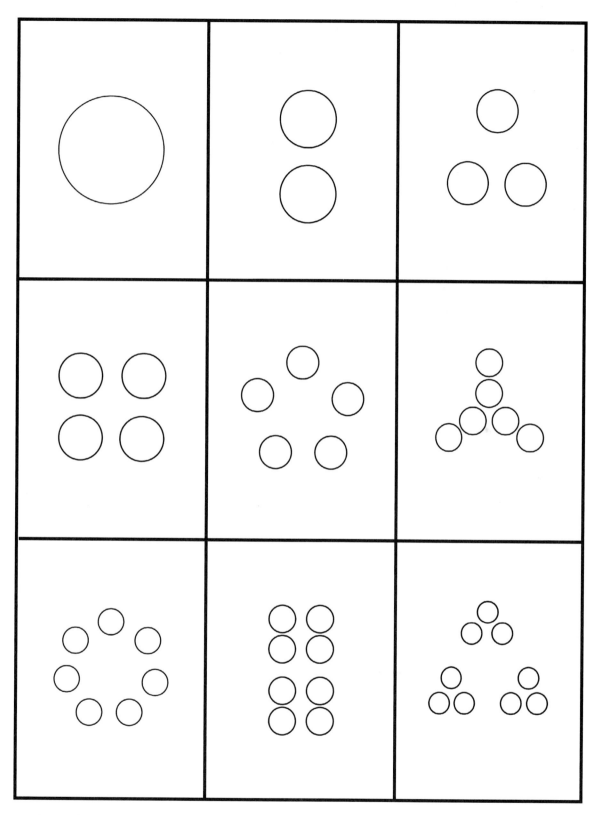

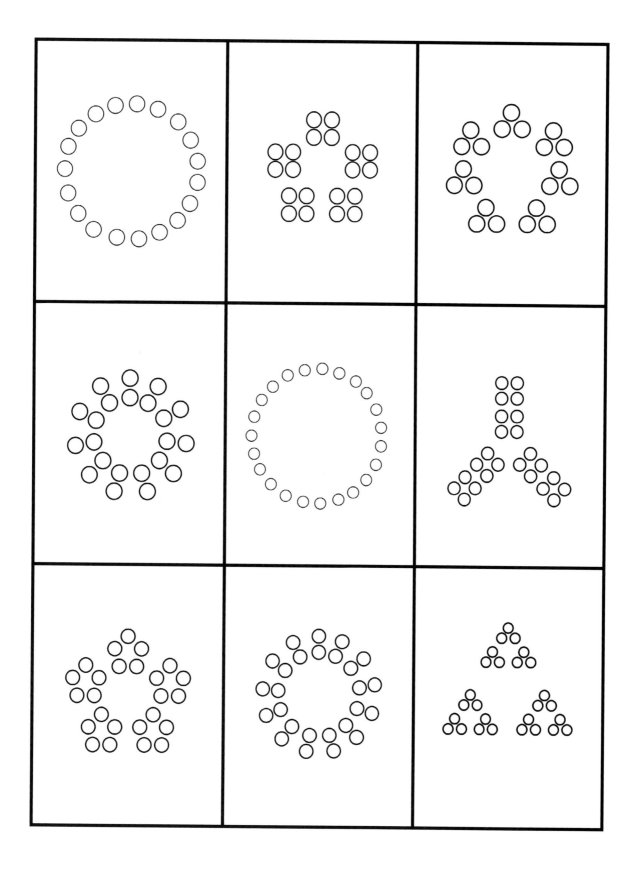

Mindset Mathematics, Grade 4, copyright © 2017 by Jo Boaler, Jen Munson, Cathy Williams.
Reproduced by permission of John Wiley & Sons, Inc.

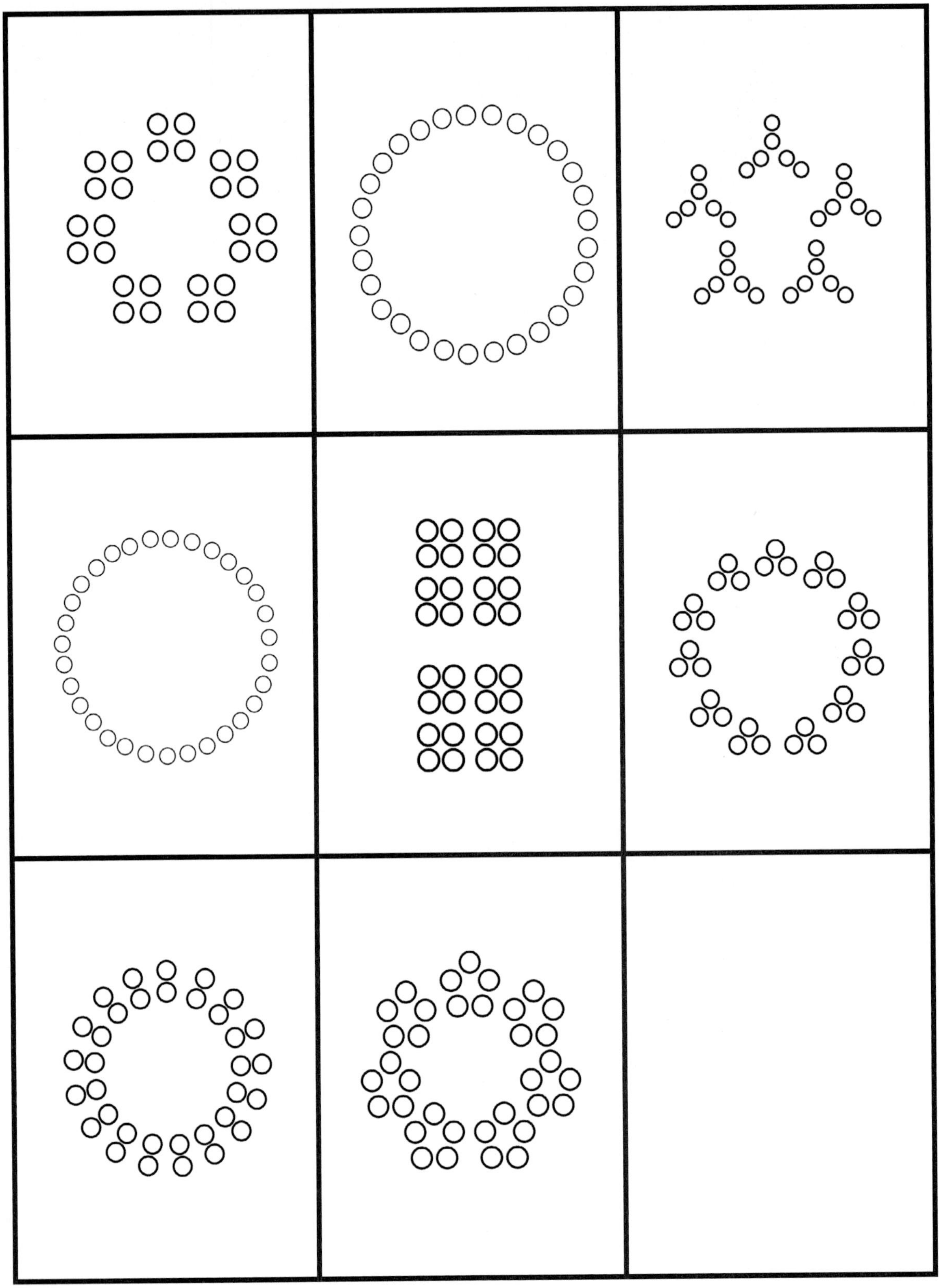

Building and Designing with Shapes and Angles

Paul Lockhart is a mathematician who wrote a famous essay called "Lockhart's Lament," in which he reflected on the mismatch between school mathematics and real mathematics. The latter, he argued, is artistic and beautiful, but the former is rote, procedural, and boring. In his book *Measurement,* Lockhart talks about the imaginary world of mathematics that is different from the real world. In the real world, he says, objects expand in different temperatures, and any measurement is only an approximation. But in the imaginary world of mathematics, all shapes are perfect— you can draw a perfect circle that you may never find in nature, and you can hold the idea of a perfect circle in your mind. This is what mathematicians love about mathematics: it has a simple beauty. Lockhart (2012) reflects that mathematics is "a beautiful wonderland of my own creation, and I can explore it and think about it and talk about it with my friends" (p. 2). The mathematics that Paul Lockhart knows is a playful world in which he meets patterns and shapes and becomes inspired to ask questions and to conduct deep inquiry. In this big idea, we introduce students to this world, inviting them to explore with different shapes, using them to make patterns and tiles that help them see the different relationships that are revealed.

In the Visualize activity, students will explore tiling by looking at some tiles from their environment and then tiling with different shapes. This is an opportunity for students to explore with different shapes, get to know them, and learn the mathematical principle of tiling. Students can also think and talk about the angles and dimensions of the shapes as they consider which shapes tile and which do not.

In the Play activity, students are introduced to a fascinating mathematical phenomenon, which is called a rep-tile. This is a type of shape that mathematicians study and that fascinate children. Students will have the opportunity to explore with creativity as they examine this mathematical phenomenon. They can again think about mathematical properties such as symmetry, parallel lines, and angles. It is fascinating to think that for any natural number above 1 (let's call it n), there is a tile that can be made where n copies of the tile can be fitted together to create a similar, larger figure. This idea should pique students' curiosity and give them the incentive to find many different shapes that are rep-tiles.

In the Investigate activity, students will meet another curious mathematical phenomenon: a polyiamond, which is a shape made out of equilateral triangles. Different types of polyiamonds can be made, and students will be invited to find as many as they can and to explore new shapes of their own. Students will need to keep organized records of the shapes they create. This is an opportunity to teach students about recording, which is an important part of being mathematical. As students record their findings in an organized way, they will also begin to see patterns. We have included questions about perimeter and area. If students see patterns as growing cases where there is one shape in the first case, two in the second, and so on, you can also make connections to multiplication and division. Students can choose a hexiamond, for example, and increase the number of shapes each time as the case number grows. Then they can determine the number of equilateral triangles in the 12th case as well as the number of the base hexiamond shape. These activities are built to provide students—and you—with opportunities to explore freely and move beyond the questions that we have included. Encourage students' creativity and exploration and talk to them about the creativity and opportunities for deep inquiry within mathematics.

Jo Boaler

Tile It!

Snapshot

In this activity, students explore which shapes tile and which shapes do not. By focusing on how shapes fit together, students begin to attend to angles as much as to sides.

Connection to CCSS
4.MD.5
4.G.1
4.G.2

Agenda

Activity	Time	Description/Prompt	Materials
Launch	5 min	Introduce students to the idea of tiling using pictures of your school environment.	Photos or local examples of tiling designs, including one with a single shape repeated and one with multiple shapes.
Explore	30+ min	Students explore tiling with single and multiple shapes, recording their findings about what shapes tile and which ones don't.	• Shape set, copied onto card stock and cut out. Each table or group will need multiple copies of each shape. • Blank paper.
Discuss	15 min	Students share their findings about shapes that do and do not tile, and the class discusses the role that angles play.	Tape, magnets, or pushpins to post student findings.

To the Teacher

This activity uses shapes to uncover ideas about angles and their relationships. We focus on the idea of *tiling*, also known as *tessellating*, in which two-dimensional shapes fit together repeatedly and infinitely in a plane. When shapes tile, they cover a plane with no gaps or overlaps. For example, squares can tile (see Figure 2.1), as can rectangles and many other shapes. Some shapes do not tile on their own, as with regular octagons. No matter how you position regular octagons, there will always be gaps. Sometimes, two or more shapes together can tile, as with regular octagons and squares (see Figure 2.2). Tiling depends on the sum of the angles around the vertex where the shapes come together. The sum must equal 360 degrees—the number of degrees in a circle—for the shapes to tile around that point. This is why squares and rectangles, with 90-degree angles, can tile easily, with four of these angles coming together. In this lesson, students will begin to explore with their eyes and hands how various angles do—and do not—fit together.

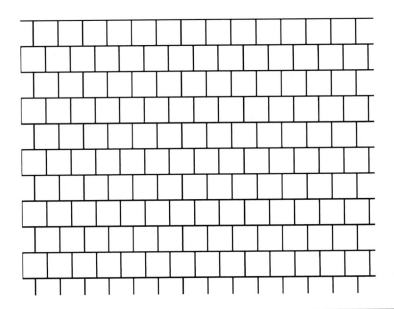

Figure 2.1   Square Tiling

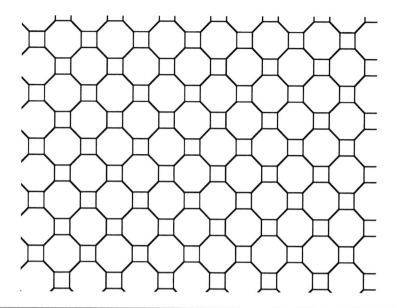

Figure 2.2   Octagon and Square Tiling

Activity

Launch

Introduce students to the idea of tiling by sharing some photos of tiled floors or surfaces. If your school has any tiled floors, you may want to include a photo or go out together and look. Ask students what they notice about how the tiles fit together. They may notice that they fit close together and that they don't overlap with each other. Tell students that we call each of the shapes a *tile,* meaning that it fits together repeatedly with no gaps or overlap. In mathematics, we say that these shapes are a *tessellation* when they cover a flat surface with no gaps or overlaps. Some shapes tessellate, and others don't. Why? Today, we're going to explore this question and see what we can find out.

Explore

Students work in groups to explore and share materials. Provide each group with several copies of the shape set and blank paper for recording their findings. Ask students to use the shapes in their shape set to explore the following questions?

- Which shapes can tile on their own? Which shapes can't?
- Which groups of shapes can tile together? Which can't?
- What happens when shapes don't tile?

For each design students try, they should record their findings, capturing which shapes tile across a surface and which shapes do not. If the shapes are printed on card stock, students can trace and reuse the shapes. Otherwise, students can tape them down, but they will then need more copies of the shapes to work with.

Discuss

Bring students back together with their findings on paper. You may want to have students create a quick display by posting their findings in categories—for example, single shapes that tile, single shapes that don't tile, multiple shapes that tile, and multiple shapes that don't tile. Ask students to look at all the findings, and ask, What do you notice?

Prompt students to look back on the shapes that don't tile. Ask, What happened when you tried to make them tile? Students will likely say that the shapes didn't fit. Encourage them to be precise about what doesn't fit. This is an opportunity to have a rich discussion about angles.

If students found that a shape tiles when with a particular partner shape but not with others, focus students' attention on this. Ask, why do you think this is? This is another opportunity for students to consider the role that angles play in tiling.

Look-Fors

- **Do students appear to understand the meaning of tiling?** Are they trying to put shapes together in repeating patterns or simply making bigger shapes (like a house)? You may want to revisit the example pictures you showed at the beginning of class to anchor students in the activity's goals.
- **How much evidence do students seem to need that the pattern can be continued?** Some students may quickly decide on the basis of only a few shapes fitting together that the shapes do or do not tile. How can they be sure? Others may need to see the pattern extend in all directions before deciding. You might want to probe, What are the cues that the pattern will continue?
- **When students find that some shapes don't tile, ask why.** Listen to the language students use to indicate the part of the shape that doesn't fit. You may want to name this part as the angle if students are struggling to find a name. You might want to collect their language (for example, "point," "end," "corner") to share with the class in the discussion and connect to the idea of angles then.

Reflect

Why do you think some shapes tile and others don't?

Shape Set

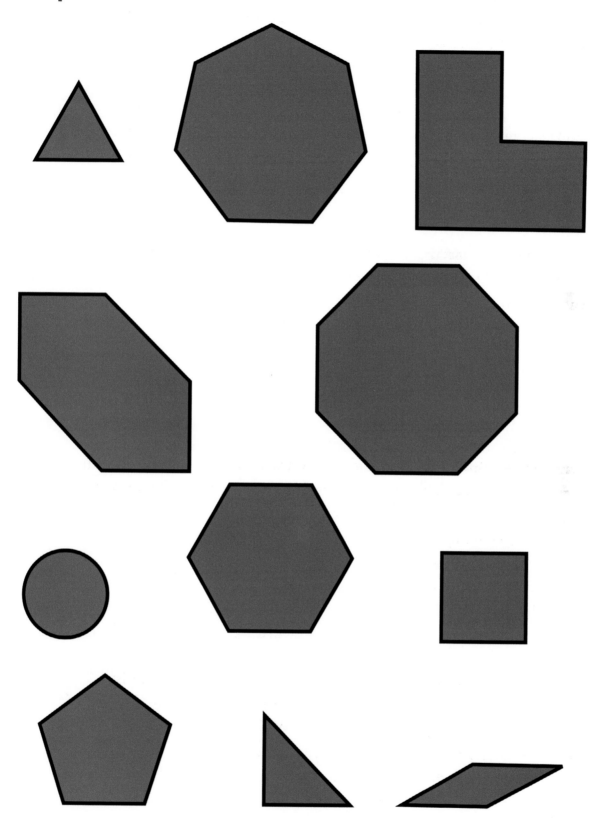

Mindset Mathematics, Grade 4, copyright © 2017 by Jo Boaler, Jen Munson, Cathy Williams. Reproduced by permission of John Wiley & Sons, Inc.

Those Crazy Rep-Tiles

Snapshot

In the previous activity, students explored tiling a plane. In this activity, we focus on special shapes that when tiled produce the shape of the base unit. These shapes are called rep-tiles. These rep-tiles are interesting to mathematicians, and they provide students a creative idea to explore.

Connection to CCSS
4.MD.5
4.G.1
4.G.2
4.G.3

Agenda

Activity	Time	Description/Prompt	Materials
Launch	10 min	Show students the visual of how shapes tile. Ask students to discuss similarities and differences in the patterns that are shown. You may want to include a discussion about symmetry, the sum of the angles at a vertex, parallel lines, perpendicular lines, etc. A question to pose is to the students is, Can these patterns continue?	• Tiling the Plane visual • Copy of Those Crazy Rep-Tiles task sheet, to show students
Play	20 min	Give students the Those Crazy Rep-Tiles task sheet and ask them to work in groups as they look for other shapes that are rep-tiles. The first task for them will be to study the diagram and determine the characteristics of a rep-tile. As students are working, you may want to stop them at an appropriate time for a class discussion about determining the definition of a rep-tile. Let students work out a class definition. If they are challenged, they can use the Internet to help.	• Those Crazy Rep-Tiles task sheet • Optional: pattern blocks • Dot paper (see appendix) • Isometric dot paper(see appendix)

Discuss	10 min	Discuss with students the strategies they developed and the challenges they faced when trying to find shapes that are rep-tiles. What strategies did they use? What are the characteristics of rep-tiles?	

To the Teacher

In this activity, students explore geometric shapes that tile and form a similar shape to the base shape, the rep-tile. These geometric shapes have different rep-tile numbers that are based on how many of the rep-tiles are needed to form the first similar shape. For any natural number $n > 1$, a tile exists where n copies of the tile can be fitted together to create a larger similar figure. On the Those Crazy Rep-Tiles task sheet, there are three shapes that are shown as examples. Each of these shapes have a rep-tile number of 4. The rep-tile number is 4 because four of the tiles are needed to form a similar shape. Can you and your students find other shapes for other natural numbers?

Activity

Launch

Show the class the Tiling the Plane visual. In this visual, students will see four examples of shapes that tile the plane. At this time, you can pose questions like these:

- What does it mean for a shape to tile?
- What are some examples of shapes that don't tile?
- What is the relationship of the angles of a shape that can tile?
- What are the similarities and differences in these four examples?

Tell students that today they are going to play with a different way of fitting shapes together. Show students the Those Crazy Rep-Tiles sheet, and ask them how these shapes are fitting together. You may want to have the turn and talk to a partner about what they notice. Draw students' attention to how the shapes fit together to make a larger, similar shape. Ask students, How do these work? Will all shapes create a rep-tile?

Play

Give students the Those Crazy Rep-Tiles task sheet and ask them to play with these rep-tiles and test their ideas by making their own. Students explore the following questions:

- Can you find other examples of shapes that are rep-tiles?
- What are the characteristics of the angle measures of shapes that are rep-tiles?
- What are the characteristics of a rep-tile?
- Is every shape a rep-tile?
- Do rep-tiles have lines of symmetry?

Students may go in different directions during their time studying the rep-tiles. Graph and isometric dot paper (see appendix) are good options for students as they explore these shapes.

Discuss

When students have had a chance to gather some ideas, bring the class together so that they can discuss what they have discovered:

- What are the characteristics of a rep-tile?
- Did you find shapes that needed a different number of tiles to form a similar shape? (The examples on the task sheet all required four tiles to make a similar shape.)
- What types of shapes did you explore?
- What types of strategies for finding rep-tiles have you come up with?
- How many rep-tiles do you think are possible?
- How do you think rep-tiles are used? Have you seen any examples of rep-tiles outside of class?

Look-Fors

- **Do students stay focused on common shapes like triangles, quadrilaterals, pentagons, and hexagons? Do they start to experiment with nonstandard shapes like the L-shaped example on the task sheet?** Encourage students to explore both regular polygons and irregular polygons. Some students may want to stick with the kinds of shapes we typically see in pattern blocks, but this set of shapes can generate misleading conclusions. Prompt students to test their ideas with irregular polygons.
- **Are students understanding that tiling means that the shape angles that join at a vertex must equal 360 degrees?** Students may not know how to measure the angles yet, but they may communicate their emerging understanding by gesturing to the vertices and circling around the point to show why the shapes fit together. They may have lots of informal language for talking about this fit. Push students to become more precise about what they mean, even if they cannot yet measure the angles. It is enough for students to describe how the angles fit around a point in a circle.
- **Do students turn and flip shapes, or do they keep them in the same orientation?** Many shapes can create rep-tiles, as with the L-shaped hexagon in the example, if the shapes are flipped or turned to fit them together. Sometimes students don't think to use these transformations and struggle to imagine what the shapes will look like when turned or flipped over. Encourage students to cut out their own shapes and move them around.

Reflect

Why do you think mathematicians study rep-tiles?

Tiling the Plane

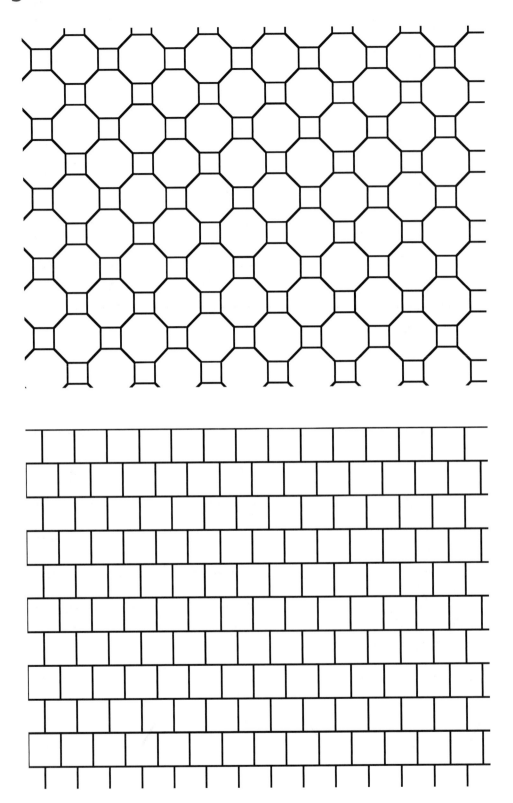

Those Crazy Rep-Tiles

Here are some interesting shapes that tile. These special shapes are called rep-tiles.

Can you find other examples of shapes that are rep-tiles?

What are the characteristics of the angle measures of shapes that are rep-tiles?

What are the characteristics of a rep-tile?

Is every shape a rep-tile?

Do rep-tiles have lines of symmetry?

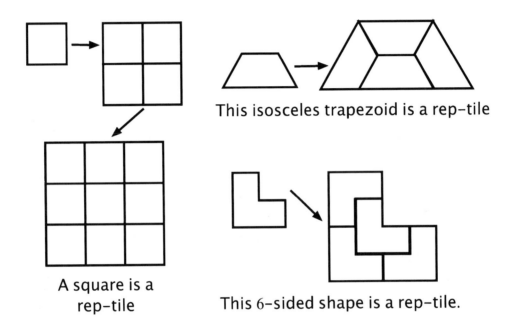

A square is a rep-tile

This isosceles trapezoid is a rep-tile

This 6-sided shape is a rep-tile.

Polyiamonds

Snapshot

In this investigation, students explore shapes made out of equilateral triangles, which are known as polyiamonds. Students will investigate the following questions: How many different shapes can you make using a set number of equilateral triangles? Will the shapes you make tile a plane?

Connection to CCSS
4.G.1
4.G.2

Agenda

Activity	Time	Description/Prompt	Materials
Launch	10 min	Ask students to draw and name different triangles. Discuss the characteristics of the different triangles.	• Equilateral triangle • Triangles from pattern block set or cut out from our set of equilateral triangles
Explore	20 min	Give students the Polyiamonds task sheet and ask them to work in groups as they create polyiamonds. Students can draw the shapes using the triangular dot paper, and/or they can build the shapes by cutting out the triangles that are provided.	• Polyiamonds task sheet • Isometric dot paper (see appendix) • Optional: set of equilateral triangles and scissors, or triangles from pattern block set
Discuss	10 min	Discuss with students the strategies they developed and the challenges they faced when trying to find shapes that are polyiamonds. What strategies did they use? What are the characteristics of a polyiamond? How do the area and perimeter change when working with different polyiamonds?	Chart and markers

(Continued)

Activity	Time	Description/Prompt	Materials
Extend	30+ min	Use a shape other than an equilateral triangle to create a series of shapes like polyiamonds. How do you know you have found all of the shapes?	• Polyiamond recording sheet, one per partnership • Square or isometric dot paper (see appendix)

To the Teacher

A polyiamond is a group of shapes in which the base shape is an equilateral triangle. In this investigation, students explore the different polyiamonds that are made up of different numbers of equilateral triangles. Students work to determine all of the different possible shapes that can be made with 2, 3, 4, 5, and 6 equilateral triangles. The equilateral triangles, when joined, must share an edge; they cannot be joined at a vertex alone. These polyiamonds are named by the number of equilateral triangles used to build them. For instance, *mon*iamonds are made with one shape, *di*amonds are made with two shapes, and so forth.

In this activity, we ask students to build as many *different* shapes as they can with the different numbers of equilateral triangles. For this activity, shapes are the same if one can be rotated or flipped and it is congruent to the other. The two hexiamonds in Figure 2.3 are different because one cannot be flipped or turned so that it is congruent to the other.

Figure 2.3 Two Examples of the Six-Triangle Group, Called *Hexiamonds*

Activity

Launch

Launch this activity by reminding students of the work they did with rep-tiles, where they joined copies of shapes to make larger, similar shapes. In this activity, students play with a variety of shapes, such as squares, triangles, and L-shaped hexagons. You might ask students what they learned about the kinds of shapes that make rep-tiles. Tell students that today they are going to work with one kind of shape. Show an image of an equilateral triangle, and ask students to turn and talk to a partner about what they notice about this shape. Collect some student observations; students will likely name this shape as a triangle and may notice that its sides are the same length. They may also notice that the angles are equal. As students make their observations, ask students to come up with a nonexample. For instance, if students say that this triangle has three equal sides, ask students to come to the board or chart to draw a triangle that does not have three equal sides.

Tell students that today they are going to be using copies of this equilateral triangle to make new shapes. Ask students, If you have one of these triangles, what shapes can you make? What if you have two? If you have three copies of this triangle, what shapes can you make? What if you have four? five? six? These shapes are called *polyiamonds.* You may want to take five or six triangles from a pattern block set and show students a couple of ways to make a polyiamond. Be sure students understand that they must join the shapes along edges so that the edges fully align. Tell students that they are going to be trying to figure out how many different shapes they can make out of the pieces, and clarify what it means to be a *different* shape.

Explore

Students work in partners using a Polyiamonds recording sheet and isometric dot paper (see appendix). Students may also want to cut out copies of the triangles from the sheet provided, or use equilateral triangles from a pattern block set. Students investigate the following questions:

- How many different shapes can you make tiling with two equilateral triangles?
- How many different shapes can you make tiling with three equilateral triangles?

- How many different shapes can you make tiling with four, five, and six equilateral triangles?
- How do you know you have found them all?

Students can also investigate what might happen with more shapes. Be advised that the number of polyiamonds that can be made increases, and the shapes become even more intricate. Encourage curious students who have already investigated using up to six equilateral triangles to try making shapes with seven, eight, and nine triangles.

Discuss

Gather students together with their findings to discuss the following questions. Chart their findings on a class table once you agree on how many polyiamonds can be made for each number of equilateral triangles.

- How many different polyiamonds did you find using 2, 3, 4, 5, and 6 equilateral triangles? Share examples of all of them.
- What names did you give your shapes?
- How do you know you have found them all?
- Were there some that were harder to find than others? Why?
- Can you tile with a hexiamond?
- Look at the table. How many polyiamonds do you predict could be made from seven triangles? eight? Why?
- How do you think your findings would change if we used a triangle that was not equilateral?

Extend

Use a different shape other than an equilateral triangle to create a series of shapes like polyiamonds. How do you know you have found all possible shapes? Does your shape make more or fewer different shapes than the equilateral triangle? Or does it make the same number? Students will need another Polyiamonds recording sheet and additional paper on which to draw. Depending on the shapes they create, students might need isometric or square dot paper (see appendix).

Look-Fors

- **Do students record their work in an organized way?** Keeping track of the possibilities becomes increasingly challenging as more equilateral triangles are used. Encourage students to think about how they will record and label the shapes they have made to make it easier to count them and to see if they are different from one another.

- **How do students record the shapes they have found?** Do they find shapes that are congruent but that they think are different because they are flipped or rotated? Some students find it very challenging to mentally flip or rotate images and consider what they will look like once transformed. Students may well need to manipulate these figures manually to test if they are different or congruent. Encourage students to rotate their papers or to flip them over and hold them up to the light. They might do better to build them out of shapes they can pick up and move. Each time students build a new polyiamond, they should test whether it is truly different.

Reflect

When you are finding shapes made up of other shapes, how can you know you found them all?

Reference

Lockhart, P. (2012) *Measurement*. Cambridge, MA: Harvard University Press.

Polyiamonds

- Polyiamonds are a set of unique shapes that are formed by tiling equilateral triangles. The table below shows the names of different polyiamonds.

- How many different shapes can you make tiling with two equilateral triangles?

- How many different shapes can you make tiling with three equilateral triangles?

- How many different shapes can you make tiling with four, five and six equilateral triangles?

- How do you know you have found them all?

The shapes made by using a set number of equilateral triangles are listed below. Can you determine how many different shapes can be made?

Polyiamond	Number of Equilateral Triangles	Number of Shapes That Can Be Formed
Moniamond	1	
Diamond	2	
Triamond	3	
Tetriamond	4	
Pentiamond	5	
Hexiamond	6	
Find some of your own		

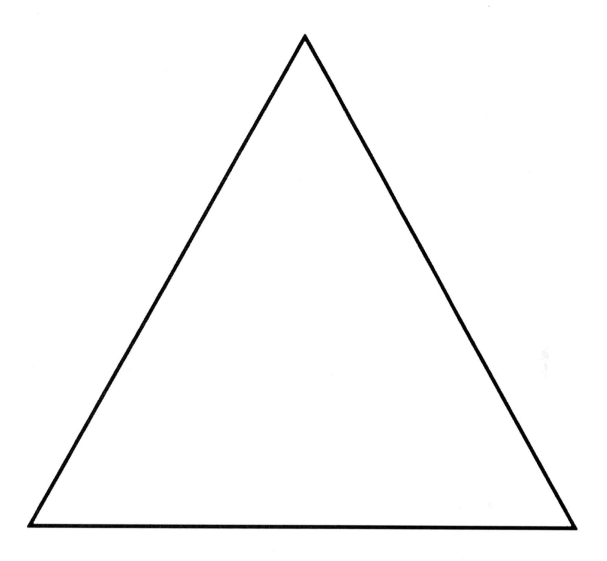

Mindset Mathematics, Grade 4, copyright © 2017 by Jo Boaler, Jen Munson, Cathy Williams.
Reproduced by permission of John Wiley & Sons, Inc.

Making and Naming Number Patterns

If you ask most schoolchildren to define mathematics, they will talk about numbers, rules, and methods. Intriguingly, if you ask mathematicians to define mathematics, many of them will say it is "the science of patterns." I think this is a really interesting statement, especially because the mathematicians are not talking about finding particular patterns such as Figure 3.1 to study.

Figure 3.1

They are talking about the way they approach mathematics and the world, and how they see every mathematical relationship as a kind of pattern. I like this way of seeing mathematics. Here is an example: you can show students that every time you divide by one half, the number you end up with will be twice as big. You can state this as a fact, or you can encourage students to see this as a kind of pattern, something that always happens, a relationship. Students who approach mathematics as a form of pattern seeking—looking for the patterns that exist between numbers and operations and seeing consistencies as a form of pattern, not a rule—often enjoy mathematics more and start to see patterns all around them.

The activities in this big idea all encourage students to be pattern seekers and to appreciate the beauty and value in patterns. This could be a good time to talk to students about the importance of patterns to mathematics, and tell them about mathematicians such as Keith Devlin and his book *Mathematics: The Science of Patterns*.

In the Visualize activity, students will explore a very famous pattern that exists all through nature and in art: the Fibonacci sequence. This activity gives students the opportunity not only to explore the number pattern but also to see it visually and be asked to extend it and make general statements about it. The act of generalizing is central to mathematics, and this is an opportunity for students to learn to generalize.

In the Play activity, students will build on their understanding of the Fibonacci pattern by making their own patterns. This will give them an opportunity to think for themselves and to act with agency. In many studies of students learning mathematics, it has been found that students who believe they have agency—the power to make their own decisions, use their own thoughts, and be autonomous—engage differently with mathematics, enjoy it more, and learn more effectively. All students at all ages need times when they work with agency, and mathematics classrooms often present too few of these opportunities to students. Asking students to make their own pattern offers them a time of agency, when they will enjoy using their own creativity, their own thinking, and their new pattern-seeking behavior.

In the Investigate activity, students will explore a famously unsolved mathematics problem, called the Collatz conjecture. This is a number sequence that all students will understand and that mathematicians have been trying to prove for decades. This may be a good time to talk about proof and what it means in mathematics. Your students may think that trying a few numbers and seeing the same result proves that something will always happen, but that is not what is meant by mathematical proof. In mathematics, we need to show that something is always true for it to be proven; a proof sometimes can be a simple diagram, and sometimes a linked set of logical statements. Mathematicians have failed to prove that these number sequences will always return to 1, although they have not yet found an instance that did not return to 1. You may want to introduce the Collatz conjecture as a challenge to students: Can they find a number that doesn't make 1? Nobody ever has, but perhaps they can? Students love to take on a challenge.

This is also a good time to introduce students to the language of conjectures. A conjecture in mathematics is like a theory in science: it is an idea that has not been proven. In my teaching, I have shared with students that it is really good to make conjectures in mathematics, and they have enjoyed learning the word and using it. The word *conjecture* helps dispel the mistaken idea that mathematics is all about certainty and helps students see that it is valuable to suggest ideas that they are not sure about—to make conjectures.

In their investigation of the Collatz conjecture, students will also be encouraged to make their own conjectures and to take their explorations of the famous conjecture to many different levels.

Students will also continue to link mathematics with nature, as they started to do in their explorations of the Fibonacci pattern. In the investigation, they will learn that the Collatz conjecture is known as the "hailstone sequence," as it models the behavior of hailstones. The different connections between mathematics and nature that are made possible in the three activities of this unit will inspire students to see mathematics as useful and engaging.

Jo Boaler

Finding Fibonacci

Snapshot

Students begin their work with patterns by exploring the Fibonacci sequence and finding connections between numerical and visual representations of the pattern.

Connection to CCSS
4.OA.5

Agenda

Activity	Time	Description/Prompt	Materials
Launch	10–12 min	Introduce the Fibonacci sequence and invite students to find the pattern. Introduce the spiral and ask students to connect it to the sequence.	Fibonacci sequence on board or chart
Explore	20 min	Students work to find connections between the Fibonacci sequence and the Fibonacci Spiral. Students then try to extend both the sequence and the visual.	• Fibonacci Spiral, one per partnership • Additional dot paper (see appendix), scissors, tape, compass, and rulers, as needed • Colors
Discuss	10–15 min	Discuss the connection between the sequence, the rule, and the visual.	
Extend	15+ min	Explore images of nature to find the Fibonacci pattern.	Fibonacci images, one or more for each partnership

To the Teacher

The Fibonacci pattern is a famous number sequence that was first introduced by Leonardo of Pisa, known as Fibonacci, in 1202. The sequence begins with 1 and 1. Then each number after these is the sum of the two previous numbers in the pattern.

The first numbers are 1 and 1, so the next member is 2 (the sum of 1 and 1), and the next is 3 (the sum of 1 and 2). The pattern can continue forever in this way, as shown in Figure 3.2. The pattern is particularly powerful because it is found throughout nature, including in the structure of pinecones, the pattern of seeds in a sunflower, and the population growth of animals. One familiar image of Fibonacci in nature is a nautilus spiral, shown in Figure 3.3, in which squares with Fibonacci side lengths are stacked in a spiral. Each square is placed next to the previous two squares, making its side length the sum of the side lengths of the previous two. This is a representation of the Fibonacci pattern we will explore in this lesson.

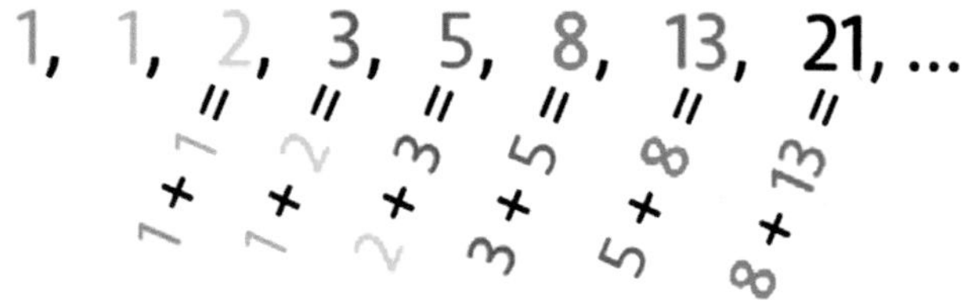

1, 1, 2, 3, 5, 8, 13, 21, ...
1 + 1 = 2
1 + 2 = 3
2 + 3 = 5
3 + 5 = 8
5 + 8 = 13
8 + 13 = 21

Figure 3.2

13
8
2
1
1
5
3
1, 1, 2, 3, 5, 8, 13

Figure 3.3

BIG IDEA 3: MAKING AND NAMING NUMBER PATTERNS

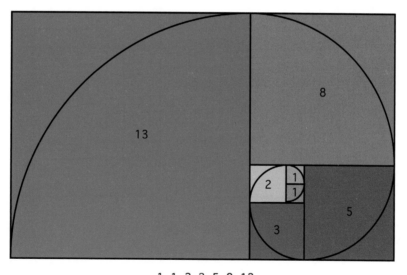

Activity

Launch

First we want students to have the opportunity to look at the Fibonacci sequence numerically and try to identify the pattern. Show students the first seven numbers of the sequence on the board or a chart: 1, 1, 2, 3, 5, 8, 13, . . . Tell students that this is a famous pattern that can be found in nature, and we continue to find more and more examples of it in our world. Ask students, What is happening in this pattern? What do you notice? Can you predict what the next number will be? Ask students to turn and talk to a partner about these questions. Ask students to share their ideas in a way that is similar to the structure of a number talk (Humphreys & Parker, 2015; Parrish 2010): What number do you think comes next and why? Scribe student ideas on the board or chart along with the reasoning. Now share with students the Fibonacci spiral for the first seven values of the sequence (Figure 3.4).

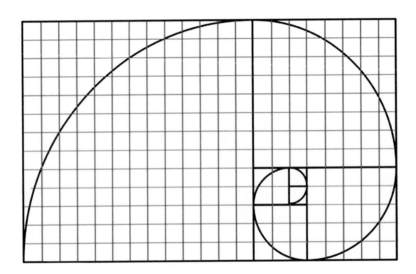

Figure 3.4

How does this picture show the sequence? Ask students to work with a partner or small group to try to match the picture to the sequence. For whatever relationships students find, they should label the picture to make them clear. Can you extend the Fibonacci sequence in the picture? With the numbers? Go as far as you can.

Explore

Ask students to work in partners with copies of the Fibonacci Spiral sheet to find the pattern and extend it. Students may want to use colors to better see each square and the visual pattern. Students may need additional dot paper (see appendix) to cut out and tape on if they make the spiral large. Encourage students to label the work they do and to extend both the picture and the number sequence as they go.

Discuss

Bring students together to share, and discuss the following questions:

- What is the Fibonacci sequence? How does it work?
- How does the spiral represent the sequence?
- How can you predict what will come next using the sequence? Using the picture?

Have students share the ways that they labeled and extended the Fibonacci spiral. You may want to open up discussion of where this spiral occurs in nature and see if students can recognize the possibilities. What does this spiral remind you of? Where might you see this kind of structure in nature?

Extend

Fibonacci shows up in many places in nature, some of which we can see in photographs or diagrams. Share the photos of the sunflower, pinecone, and cactus, and ask students to investigate: Where is Fibonacci? Students can mark up their own copies of the pictures to count, segment, and hunt for the pattern. Figure 3.5 shows some examples of where they might see Fibonacci in these photos, but there are many more that students might find.

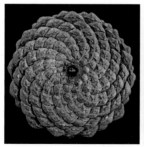  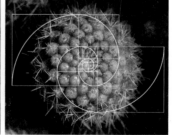

a. Fibonacci in a pinecone. There are 13 spirals.

b. Fibonacci in a sunflower. There are 34 spirals.

c. Fibonacci patterns in a cactus.

Figure 3.5

Look-Fors

- **Are students attending to how the numbers grow?** Students may have experience only with repeating patterns (like AB patterns), but the patterns that will support algebraic thinking are those that grow. You'll want to draw students' attention to the change between members of the pattern. The values in the pattern don't grow consistently, as when we count by 5s. Instead, the jumps between numbers are also growing because each new number (or square) must be as big as the two previous ones combined. All of these layers of patterns mean that it is much more challenging for students to see and hold on to a pattern like Fibonacci than an AB pattern or a skip-counting pattern.

- **Are students making connections between the visual and the numbers?** In the spiral, students may be tempted to focus on the area of the squares being created, rather than the side lengths. You may need to focus students on the question, Where is the sequence in this picture?

- **Are students labeling their picture in ways that help them focus on patterning?** Labels can help students construct the next elements in the spiral, each of which needs to be a square to maintain the pattern.

Reflect

How did the visual pattern help you understand the number sequence? How did the number sequence help you understand the visual pattern?

Fibonacci Spiral

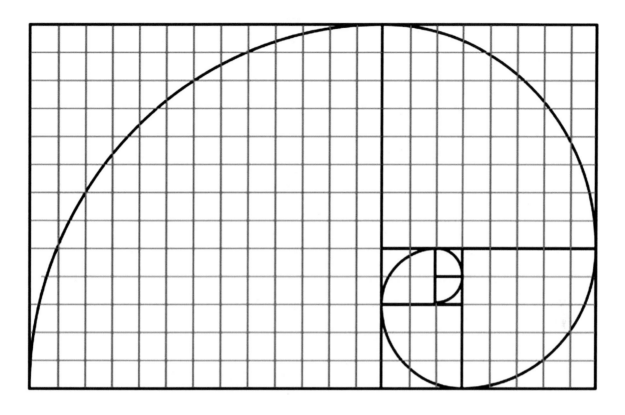

Mindset Mathematics, Grade 4, copyright © 2017 by Jo Boaler, Jen Munson, Cathy Williams.
Reproduced by permission of John Wiley & Sons, Inc. Image by Shutterstock.com/Violart.

Mindset Mathematics, Grade 4, copyright © 2017 by Jo Boaler, Jen Munson, Cathy Williams. Reproduced by permission of John Wiley & Sons, Inc. Image by Shutterstock.com/Bringolo.

Mindset Mathematics, Grade 4, copyright © 2017 by Jo Boaler, Jen Munson, Cathy Williams. Reproduced by permission of John Wiley & Sons, Inc. Image by Shutterstock.com/Heather Dillon.

Pattern Carnival

Snapshot

Students extend their work with number patterns and visual patterns by making their own. We use the patterns students create to hold a pattern carnival in which kids engage with the patterns others create and try to identify and extend those patterns.

> Connection to CCSS
> 4.OA.5

Agenda

Activity	Time	Description/Prompt	Materials
Launch	5 min	Remind students of the two ways we saw the Fibonacci patterns, and set up expectations for creating their own patterns on posters.	Sample poster made with Fibonacci pattern
Create	30+ min	Students work with a partner to create their own patterns with numbers and visuals on a poster for the carnival.	• Posters and markers for each partnership • Make available: rulers, dot paper (see appendix), colors, scissors, and tape
Play	30+ min	Students stage a pattern carnival with the posters they have created. Students circulate to try to understand and extend the patterns others have created.	• Pattern posters created by students • Clipboard and paper or notebooks for students to work in while they walk
Discuss	20 min	Discuss how students created their own patterns and the different patterns created in the class.	Pattern posters created by students

To the Teacher

This lesson can easily be spread across more than one day. In particular, you may want to create patterns on one day and hold the carnival and discussion on a second day. You'll want to think about what structure for the carnival would work best for your students and your space. We've offered two ideas in this lesson, but certainly other ways are possible.

Activity

Launch

Launch the lesson by reminding students of the work they've done with Fibonacci. A number pattern can also be represented with a picture. You may want to show the Fibonacci sequence and a spiral again. Tell students that today we are going to create our own number and visual patterns and then have a pattern carnival. Ask students to work with a partner to create patterns that can be shown both with numbers and with pictures. Some students may decide to start with the visual and translate it into numbers; others may do the opposite. Either works. For the pattern students create, ask them to show both representations on a poster without describing what the pattern is. Tell student that the class will use the posters as pattern games in a carnival. The questions the class will ask about each pattern will be: What comes next? How do you know? Encourage students to think creatively with their partner, but to keep their pattern private so that it makes a great puzzle for others.

Create

Students work with partners to create a pattern that they can show with numbers and pictures. Ask students to make a poster of their work that others can use as a puzzle, asking: What comes next? How do you know? Their poster could look like the one in Figure 3.6. You might encourage students to make it as interesting and

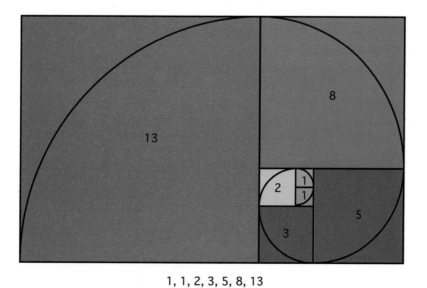

1, 1, 2, 3, 5, 8, 13

Figure 3.6   What comes next? How do you know?

attractive as possible to make the game fun, and students can choose a name for their pattern if they want. Prompt students to make their visuals as precise as possible so that the pattern is clear. Offer tools like rulers, dot or grid paper (see appendix), and colors to support this precision.

Play

Create your carnival. There are lots of ways to run your carnival. Here are just two options:

1. Game stations. Have half the partners display their posters either on the wall or at tables. These partners will stay by their posters while the other half of the class roams from poster to poster trying to figure out the patterns, working on clipboards or in notebooks. The host partners can engage students in conversations about the patterns and ask the questions: What comes next? How do you know? What do you notice? Does that work for the whole pattern? After 10–15 minutes, partner roles should flip, with the roaming partners now displaying their posters and the hosts now having a chance to roam.

2. Gallery walk. Have all students post their patterns around the room or hallway. Have all partners stand by their poster and then rotate everyone clockwise to the next poster. Give students a few minutes to look at the poster and try to figure out: What comes next? How do you know? Students can carry clipboards or notebooks to work out and record their thinking. After a few minutes, rotate everyone to the next poster. Students may or may not be able to figure out all of the patterns.

Discuss

Bring students together to discuss some of the patterns they created and explored during the carnival.

- How did you make your pattern? What was your process?
- What was challenging about making a pattern?
- What kind of patterns did you see? Are there patterns that are similar? How so? Which patterns were very different? Why?

You may want to focus discussion on one particular pattern that was difficult or unique. Alternatively, you could compare two patterns that used very different rules. You might ask questions like these:

- What comes next? How do you know?
- What is the rule for this pattern? How would we name it?
- What makes this pattern different? How would we describe those differences?

Look-Fors

- **Are students thinking creatively about the kinds of patterns they create?** Students may be tempted to simply reproduce Fibonacci, but we want them to think in different ways. If students are stuck, you might prompt them to switch how they are trying to generate the pattern, moving from numbers to visuals or vice versa.
- **Do the patterns hold across the sequence?** Students may start a pattern one way and switch the rule at some point in the sequence. Ask students probing questions about how they created each element in their patterns to ensure that they maintain consistency.
- **Do the pictures and number sequence truly match?** Ask students to show you how they match, and focus on their precision in the pattern, picture, and explanation.
- **Can students describe the rule?** Focus on getting students to clearly articulate the rule they have created.
- **Are students checking the rules they identify in others' work?** A rule may work for two elements of a pattern but not all. If that is the case, the rule doesn't accurately represent the whole pattern, and students should return to the pattern to try again.

Reflect

Choose one of these avenues to explore:

- When people came to your pattern, how did they figure it out? What did others notice in your pattern? Did they rely more on the numbers or the picture? Why do you think that is?
- What made your pattern interesting to you? To others? If you were to make another pattern, what would you do differently?

All Hail!

Snapshot

Students will explore an unsolved mathematics conjecture, called the Collatz conjecture, related to a kind of number sequence. They will make number sequences using doubling and halving strategies, and develop visual diagrams to illustrate their number sequences. Students will use the visual diagrams to make their own conjectures about this fascinating problem.

> Connection to CCSS
> 4.OA.5

Agenda

Activity	Time	Description/Prompt	Materials
Launch	10 min	Introduce students to how hailstones are formed. Introduce them to a mathematics conjecture and what it means for a problem to not yet have a proof.	How Hailstones Are Formed, to show students
Explore	30 min	Students generate hailstone sequences and explore patterns generated from their sequences. Students generalize their pattern into a conjecture and generate a visual display of their work.	• Posters and markers for each group • Optional: grid paper (see appendix)
Discuss	15 min	Students share their findings about their work and synthesize their class findings into one or more group conjectures.	
Extend	20+ min	Groups create visuals for the class conjecture to communicate their evidence.	• Posters and markers • Grid paper (see appendix)

To the Teacher

This investigation hinges on the notion of a mathematical conjecture. Be sure as you launch the lesson that students have a shared understanding of what a conjecture is so that you can use this language throughout the lesson. Conjectures are ideas that people have about mathematical connections. They are ideas that have not been proved; mathematicians cannot yet be certain that they are accurate for all possibilities. Critically, conjectures have also not yet been proven false, which means no one has yet found a case where they do not work. In the case of the hailstone sequence, this means that for all the sequences people have attempted, they all end in 1, as predicted by the Collatz conjecture. We don't yet know whether this will truly always be the case or whether there exists a case where the sequence does not end in 1 (or does not end at all).

Activity

Launch

Launch the lesson by showing students a visual of how hailstones are formed (shown in Figure 3.7 and provided as a full-page image at the end of the lesson).

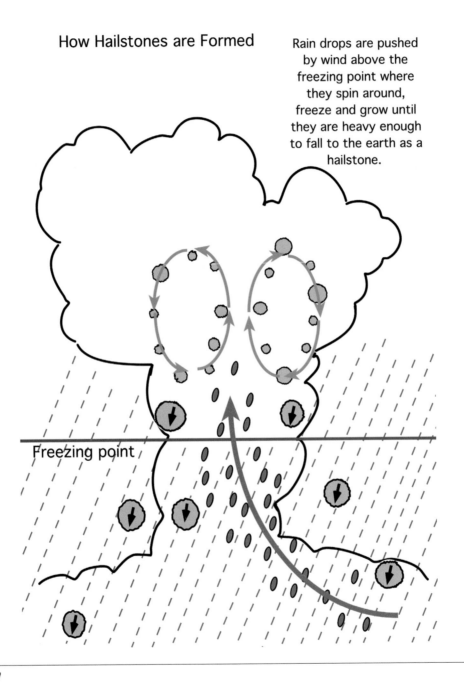

How Hailstones are Formed

Rain drops are pushed by wind above the freezing point where they spin around, freeze and grow until they are heavy enough to fall to the earth as a hailstone.

Freezing point

Figure 3.7

Hailstones start in a cloud as drops of rainwater, then are pushed higher in the atmosphere by wind, where they freeze, sometimes several times, before eventually falling back to earth. The number sequences that students are going to work on today have been called hailstone sequences because they share some of the features of hailstone behavior.

A hailstone sequence follows these rules:

- Start with any whole number.
- If the number is even, divide it by 2 (or halve it).
- If the number is odd, multiply it by 3 and add 1.
- Continue generating numbers in this way until your sequence ends.

Here's an example of a hailstone sequence: 20, 10, 5, 16, 8, 4, 2, 1.

How does a hailstone sequence end? These hailstone sequences are a problem in mathematics that still has no proof. There is a conjecture by Lothar Collatz, called the Collatz conjecture, which states that all of these hailstone sequences end with the number 1. However, this hasn't yet been proved, so it is still a conjecture. Students will study these sequences and come up with their own conjectures—ideas with evidence that can be used to make predictions—which they will share with the class. Ask students if they can find a case that doesn't end in 1. Tell students that you are going to ask them later why they think these sequences are called hailstone sequences.

Explore

Students work in partnerships or small groups to generate hailstone sequences. Students should try several different starting numbers to see what happens to the sequence. Ask students to investigate the patterns of their sequences and make a conjecture about what they discover.

Each group should make a poster to show their number sequences and findings. The poster should include a visual display of the sequences students investigated. This might include a picture, illustration, number line, graph, or any other visual way of representing the sequences so that we can better see what happens within them. The poster should also include the group's conjecture(s) about what happens in these patterns and how they end.

Discuss

Ask each group to present their poster with conjectures, number sequences, and visuals. As students present, ask the class to listen for evidence in each poster that is similar to or different from their own group's work. Students should pay attention to how all the ideas and evidence presented across the groups fit together or conflict.

After all groups have presented, lead a discussion regarding generalizing all of their findings into a class conjecture.

- What do we seem to agree on? What evidence do we have as a class to support our ideas?
- What do we disagree on? What evidence have we found that seems to conflict? How can we resolve this? Do we need any additional evidence?
- How can we revise our conjectures into one class conjecture about hailstone sequences?

Extend

Students can work in their small groups to create a visual of the class conjecture. They should consider these questions:

- How could you communicate our conjecture to someone who has not yet learned about hailstone sequences?
- What evidence could you provide to make the conjecture clear and convincing?
- How can you make your evidence visible? What kinds of visual displays or features did you find most useful or convincing in the class presentations? Why?

The class can use these questions to create a class display or bulletin board of their hailstone sequence conjecture, including how the sequences work, the conjecture, and the evidence in all forms. Student-created displays of shared mathematical work can be useful ways of communicating with others—colleagues, students, and parents—what rich mathematical thinking looks like. Conjectures like these invite others to participate by sparking wondering and puzzling over the evidence.

Look-Fors

- **Do students generate hailstone sequences with precision and accuracy?** A critical first step to investigating these patterns is accurately generating a hailstone sequence. Students will need to determine even and odd numbers and work with halving and multiplying by 3. Some students might benefit from modeling this pattern directly with blocks or on grid paper (see appendix), which will also help create visuals.

- **Do students organize their work into a format that supports the comparison of findings?**

- **Be sure to ask students how they will organize what they are finding.** There are many ways students might decide to track each pattern, but consistency will be important for comparison. Students might want to simply record the sequences as numbers, but this may mask the shape of the patterns. You may want to encourage students to make their visuals before comparing.

- **Do students synthesize their results into an accurate conjecture?** Students will need to think across several sequences to arrive at a conjecture. Then they will need to draw on evidence across their sequences to support their ideas, and they will need to investigate their sequences for counterexamples. Once student think they have a conjecture, you might encourage them to test it by generating an additional sequence to see if it gives the expected result.

- **Do students construct an accurate and creative visual display of their sequences leading to visual evidence for a conjecture?** The visual displays students create are key to seeing patterns across the sequences. Line graphs tend to be particularly useful, but many other kinds of displays may work for students: bar graphs, jumps on a number line, stacks of blocks, or something else students invent. Different sorts of labeling or color coding might also help in looking for patterns. Ask students what would help them see what is happening in their sequences, and encourage them to try out different ideas. They might discover that their initial ideas would benefit from revision. Focus students on the usefulness of the visual for themselves. It should be an effective tool. You might ask, What would make this display more useful for you?

Reflect

Why do you think these number sequences are called hailstone sequences?

References

Humphreys, C., & Parker, R. (2015). *Making number talks matter: Developing mathematical practices and deepening understanding, grades 4–10.* Portland, ME: Stenhouse.

Parrish, S. (2010). *Number talks: Helping children build mental math and computation strategies, grades K–5.* Sausalito, CA: Math Solutions.

How Hailstones Are Formed

How Hailstones are Formed

Rain drops are pushed by wind above the freezing point where they spin around, freeze and grow until they are heavy enough to fall to the earth as a hailstone.

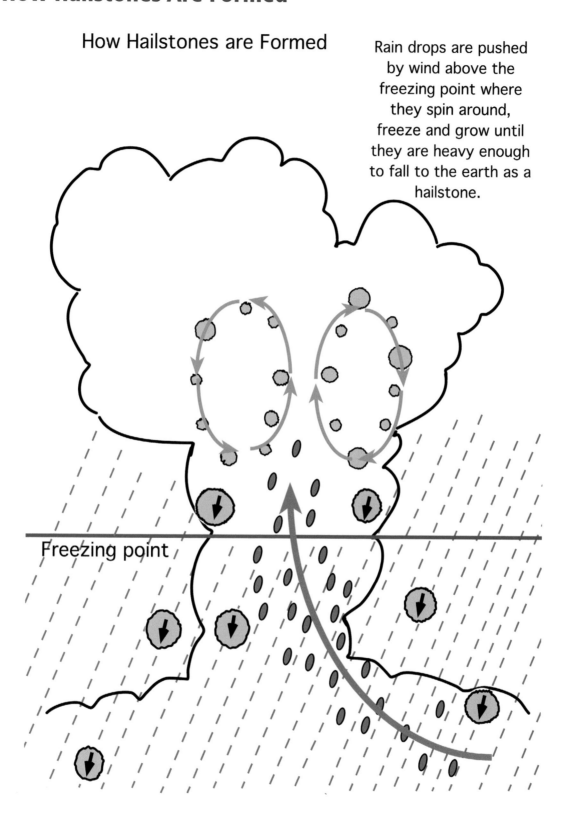

Freezing point

BIG IDEA 4

Units Are a Relationship

Our world is made up of a great variety of objects and substances, all of which are measured at different times to help us make decisions that are important to our lives. Parents need to understand measuring units when they give their children medicine, just as engineers need to understand measuring units when they build bridges or iPhones. Our world is measurable because of the many different units that have been created, and this big idea gives students an opportunity to become familiar with different units and to start to understand the ways they are related to each other. I discussed in the introduction to Big Idea 2 the imaginary world of mathematics that allows us to see and draw perfect circles. This big idea takes us into the real world, in which measurement is necessary. But measurement in the real world can never be exact, and that is a useful idea for students to understand. One of the reasons mathematics is so useful and intriguing is that it is partly imaginary, and this allows us to create perfect shapes. It is also a way we understand our world, and we use measurement to help us make sense of the world, even though they cannot be perfectly accurate.

In the Visualize activity, we invite students to think about the relationship between two units through the use of a graph. This may be the first time students have spent time with graphs, and our intention is that they work to make sense of the graphs, noting their general shape and the ways that the values on one axis relate to the values on the other. We are starting with an activity that is similar to one we used in our WIM lessons that students found very engaging. Students will be asked to look at a graph with different animals and consider what the graph is showing them. They will then be asked to make their own graphs and to reason and make conjectures about graphs. We have infused the first graphing tasks with opportunities for creativity and for students to reason and to prove their ideas. Graphs are an opportunity to see data visually, and they can be used to encourage students to think intuitively about ideas.

In our Play activity, students will use nonstandard measurements to learn more about their classroom. This is an activity that incorporates student choice, which is important to encourage wherever possible. Students will get the opportunity to choose any unit of measurement, such as a pencil or a book, and use it to measure five objects in the room, showing their results in a line plot. This is an opportunity for students to think more about measurement and to learn a new way of recording information.

In our Investigate activity, students will be asked to consider the meaning of 10,000 steps, thinking about the length they represent, the ways they may be combined, and the distances they add up to. The investigation has openness in asking students to consider where they could get to with 10,000 steps, how long it could take, and the possible destinations they could reach. The openness will be engaging for students, as they can use their imaginations to think of interesting places they may visit, at the same time using a unit of measurement and thinking deeply about it.

Jo Boaler

It's All in the Axes

Snapshot

In this activity, we make the relationship between units visible by examining and creating graphs. We use these graphs to make observations and predictions about relationships, both within and beyond the graph.

> Connection to CCSS
> 4.MD.1

Agenda

Activity	Time	Description/Prompt	Materials
Launch	15+ min	Examine the animal graph and ask students to determine what information the graph provides, what the axes mean, and what questions they have. Discuss these observations.	Animal Graph, to show students
Explore	20+ min	Students work in small groups to create their own poster graph like the animal graph studied in the launch.	Chart paper and markers
Discuss	20 min	Students study a graph that has been completed by another group. They address key questions and present the graph to the class with their findings.	For each group, a graph on chart paper completed by another group.

To the Teacher

Graphs are a particularly potent way of visualizing patterns, but to make sense of these patterns, students need to develop ways of reading and interacting with these images. We start with an examination of a graph of two variables that builds students' intuition for the relationships communicated on a graph. Graphs should be an inviting way to visualize and explore patterns and relationships, and this first experience is intended to engage students in meaning-making with the graphs before pivoting to the unit relationships at the heart of the big idea. The rest of the lesson aims to make unit relationships visible. Here we ask students to construct their own understandings of the graph and later to create their own graphs. You may see students constructing their graphs in unconventional ways. This is just fine. The only criteria should be consistency and clarity. Do the graphs communicate the relationship they intended?

An additional extension to this lesson might be to have students construct puzzles from the graphs students themselves create. These could get posted alongside the graph display to serve as ongoing puzzles for students to try out by touching or thinking about the graphs.

Activity

Launch

Tell students that today we're going to be looking for relationships. Show students the animal graph (found at the end of this activity). Ask students to turn and talk to a partner: What do you notice? What information can you gather from this visual display? Give students a few minutes to make observations of all kinds. Ask students to share aloud what they notice, and chart their contributions. You will also want to annotate your copy of the graph to show the features that students are attending to. Be sure to use colors to show different patterns or observations. You may want to choose a few animals that are not on the graph (for example, a dog or a zebra) and ask the students to turn and talk to a partner about where they would add them to the graph and why. Ask students to share their reasoning about where to place these animals on the graph. This is a useful moment for formative assessment: Are students understanding how to interpret the information in the graph?

Explore

Ask students to create their own graph, on chart paper, like the animal graph they have just studied. In their groups, they will need to decide on a topic and what the axes represent. They will need to work together to come to consensus on what they choose to do and how they create their graph. Make sure to tell them that they cannot make a graph with the same animals or axis labels as the previous animal graph.

Discuss

When students have completed their poster graphs, give each group a graph that was completed by another group. Ask each group to discuss the following questions and plan how they will share the graph with the class during the class discussion.

- What is this graph trying to communicate?
- What do the axes represent?
- What relationships are being illustrated?
- What questions do you have for the students who made the poster?

Look-Fors

- **Are students using the features of the axes to make meaning about the data shown?** There are lots of pieces of information on a graph, and weaving them together to form an interpretation of a single data point is challenging. To support students in dealing with both axes and what the data points represent, it can be useful to focus in on just a single point and ask questions about what it means.

- **Are students connecting the individual data points into an overall pattern?** Students may see the points only as individual bits of data, rather than as a pattern or a relationship. You may want to focus students on the idea of a pattern and a relationship and ask students how they could summarize what they see to someone who could not see the graph, as when talking over the phone.

- **How are students reasoning about data beyond the graph?** Students can certainly extend the graph and wonder about related items that are not on the graph. Students will need to have a sense of the relationship of the items to the axes.

- **How are students thinking about graph construction?** Graphs need some features to make them readable to others. Encourage students to think about what features made the graphs readable for them. How can they include those same features in a graph with a different pattern? The placement of items on the graph will matter.

Reflect

How do graphs communicate relationships?

Animal Graph

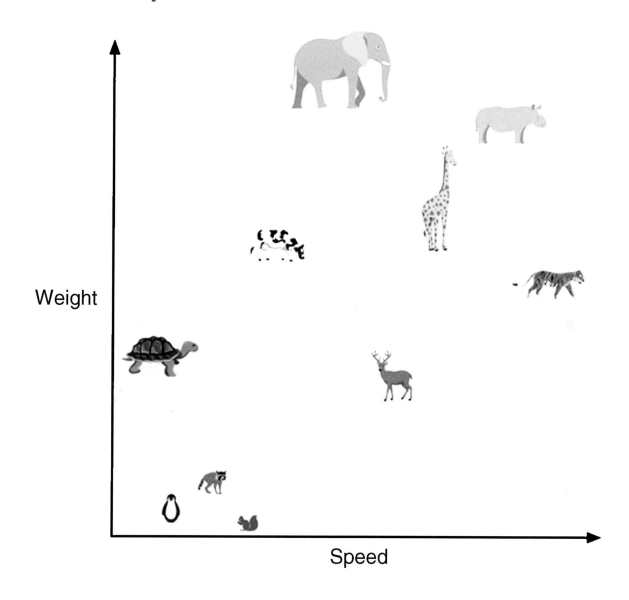

Weight

Speed

Measure Up

Snapshot

Students use a nonstandard unit of measurement to determine the size of different classroom objects.

Connection to CCSS
4.MD.1
4.MD.4

Agenda

Activity	Time	Description/Prompt	Materials
Launch	10–15 min	Show students the line plot and ask them to think about what information it communicates. As a class, discuss their observations.	• Measuring by Forks Line Plot, to show students • Copies of Measuring by Forks Line Plot, one for each partnership
Play	20 min	Ask pairs of students to choose a unit of measurement—for example, a pencil, orange Cuisenaire rod, or blue 10 block. Students create their own line plot by measuring objects in the classroom using their unit of measurement.	• Measure Up unit, such as a pencil, orange Cuisenaire rod, or whiteboard eraser • Colored pens and chart paper
Discuss	10–15 min	Ask students to display their posters. Students can move around the room studying the information shown on the line plots.	• Completed line plot posters • Sticky notes for student comments

Extend	15+ min	Ask students to convert their unit of measurement to inches, centimeters, or another appropriate standard unit of measurement. They can make a conversion table to determine the unit of measurement for their line plot. The conversion table can be displayed with their line plot poster, and questions can be posed about the standard measure for the items that were included in the line plot.	Rulers, meter sticks, yardsticks

To the Teacher

This lesson can extend across two days, particularly if you decide to do the extension activity. Students will likely learn more if given the opportunity to return to the line plot posters on other days.

In this activity, students create line plots showing the measurements of different classroom objects. The unit of measurement will be something they have chosen to use as their standard of measure. For example, a pair of students might choose a pencil and then determine how many pencils tall the door is, or their desk, or the distance across the classroom.

In the extension, students make a conversion table that can be posted with their poster. They can also craft questions about their items where other students can use the conversion table to identify the measure of the objects with a standard measure.

Activity

Launch

Launch this activity by reminding students of the work they did with the coordinate plane. Tell students that there are lots of ways to communicate information with a graph and that today we're going to look at a different sort of graph. Show students the Measuring by Forks Line Plot and give partners a copy to look at up close (Figure 4.1; the full-page version appears at the end of the lesson). Ask students to study it with their partner and determine what information it communicates. Ask students to share their findings. Record their observations in a space that is easy for all of them to see. Be sure to draw students' attention to the partial forks and ask them to speculate on what these are meant to communicate. Ask students to make their own line plots using a nonstandard unit for measuring objects in the classroom.

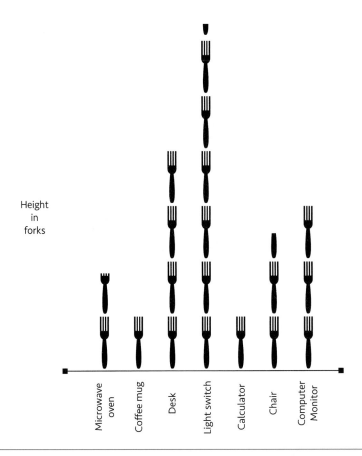

Figure 4.1

Play

Students work together in pairs to determine a nonstandard unit of measurement. For example, a group might choose a pencil, stapler, whiteboard eraser or some other classroom object. Ask students to find the measure of at least five different things in the classroom. For example, students might measure the height or width of the door, the distance across the classroom, or the height of a desk. When they have collected their information, they should illustrate their data using a line plot.

Discuss

Ask students to display their posters where other students can study their line plots. Ask students to record the questions that the line plots raise, any suggestions they have for making the line plots clearer, and comments on features that are particularly interesting or clear. Students can use sticky notes to leave messages for the creators of each line plot.

Then gather the class together to discuss the following questions:

- What questions did these line plots raise for you?
- What do the line plots communicate clearly?
- What is hard to read on these line plots? Why?
- How did you (and others) make use of fractional units?

Extend

Ask students to make a table that shows the conversion of their nonstandard unit of measurement to a standard unit of measurement, similar to the example shown here. Students can display their conversion table with their line plot poster. You might then have students go around to compare the measures of the same objects across different charts to see if they agree. For instance, if the desk is four forks tall on one line plot and five pencils tall on a different line plot, are they the same height? How can the conversion charts help students to figure this out?

Number of forks	1	2	3	4	5	6	7
Height in inches	7	14	21	28	35	42	49

Look-Fors

- **Are students measuring accurately with their unit of measurement?** Students still often struggle with laying units end to end, particularly when measuring vertically. Push students to develop ways of measuring that are increasingly precise.

- **How are students addressing partial units?** Be sure to press students to think carefully about these pieces, how big they actually are, and how they will record that portion of the measurement.

- **Are the line plots accurate?** Ask students to show you their data and how they mapped this data onto the line plot. In having to explain, students may catch simple errors. Ask students if they think their measures are reasonable. For instance, if two objects are shown as equal on the line plot, do students believe they are actually equal in height?

- **How are students thinking about their conversion charts?** Again, there may be a need to think about fractional units. A pencil may be 5½ inches long, rather than 5 or 6 inches. Students should be as precise as possible and not round this conversion to a whole number. Push students to think carefully about how they will find the measure of 2, 3, 4 units and so on, to construct their tables.

Reflect

Why do you think we have so many different units of measurement in our world?

Measuring by Forks Line Plot

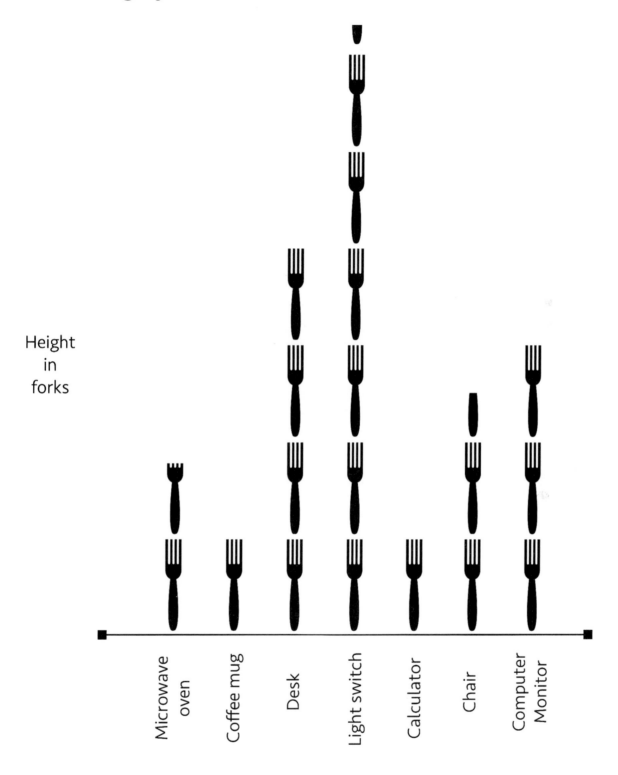

Height
in
forks

Microwave oven

Coffee mug

Desk

Light switch

Calculator

Chair

Computer Monitor

10,000 Steps

Snapshot

In this investigation, students consider how far they can travel in 10,000 steps. They also consider the amount of time it would take to walk 10,000 steps.

Connection to CCSS
4.MD.1
4.MD.2
4.OA.3

Agenda

Activity	Time	Description/Prompt	Materials
Launch	10 min	Introduce the recommendation that people walk 10,000 steps per day, and the key questions How far is this? and How long would it take you to walk that distance? Remind students of their previous work with unit relationships. Ask students to consider what information and tools they will need.	

Explore	45+ min	Students work in small groups to tackle four key questions:
		
		• If you walked 10,000 steps each day, how far would you go?
		• How long would it take you to walk all 10,000 steps at once?
		• If you walked 10,000 steps each day for a year, how far would you go?
		• How different are your answers to these questions for each member of your group?
		
		Students use tools of their own choosing to develop a solution pathway and create a poster of their process.
			• Posters and markers for each group
			• Access to:
			  • Clocks or stopwatches
			  • Meter sticks or yard-sticks
			  • Calculators
			  • Space to walk
			  • Tools to mark the floor (e.g., sticky notes or masking tape)
			  • References for unit relationships, as needed

Discuss	30 min	All groups share their approaches and results using their process posters, while the class poses questions and considers how convincing the methods used are. Students then discuss the sources of the similarities and differences in the results across the class.	Group posters
Explore	20+ min	Students investigate where they might go on a 10,000-step walk and construct a route using maps of your area.	Maps of your area, with scale indicated

To the Teacher

This investigation is like most real-world problems in that the language of the problem does not tell us what steps will be needed or what approach to use. Students will have to think creatively and systematically about how they move from the information they know toward the answers to the questions posed. Although it may be tempting to provide additional scaffolds by breaking this task into a series of smaller questions and steps, we encourage you to support students instead by asking them what they want to know and what they will need to get there. You can additionally support students by pausing the investigation after about 10 minutes and asking students to share ideas they are developing for getting started. This can spur thinking for students who are stuck. If a group is having a particularly hard time imagining how to proceed, you might offer them the opportunity to gather ideas by walking around for a few minutes as a group and listening in on the thinking that other groups are trying out. This kind of idea gathering is a strategic way of using peer models while keeping students in control of what ideas they decide to try out themselves.

Activity

Launch

Launch this investigation by reminding students about the ways in which we've been looking at unit relationships so far. The goal with unit relationships is that we can use them to solve problems and decide how to move between units. We're going to tackle that in today's challenge. Doctors are now recommending that people walk 10,000 steps each day to maintain their health and be active. Show students what we mean by a step—one typical stride. Ask students if they think they walk 10,000 steps each day. You can record their ideas and revisit their ideas after they have completed the investigation. Explain to students that we are going to investigate this idea by trying to figure out how far that is for you and how long it would take you to walk 10,000 steps. What do you think you'd need to figure out to start this investigation? Invite students to turn and talk to a partner about what sorts of things they would need to know. You might ask students to offer some ideas, such as how far a step is or how many steps it takes to go down the hallway.

Ask students to record their thinking and results on a poster. Later they will be able to see how others approached the problem. Encourage them to be organized and descriptive so that other students can understand their method and answers to the questions posed in this activity.

Explore

Students work in small groups to find a solution pathway for the following questions:

- If you walked 10,000 steps each day, how far would you go?
- How long would it take you to walk all 10,000 steps at once?
- If you walked 10,000 steps each day for a year, how far would you go?
- How different are your answers to these questions for each member of your group?

Each group should create a poster to document their process and findings. Color coding could be a useful strategy for making the different steps or stages in the process clear. There is a lot of data to be gathered in this investigation; encourage students to use their posters from the beginning to record the information they collect and what they do with it to support them in keeping track.

Students should be given access to all the measurement and reference tools they might need to gather the necessary data and calculate. Groups might decide to use different tools, so we recommend making the tools available in a central location rather than distributing them.

Note that this investigation involves a rich set of mathematical ideas about units and operations. Even more important, the challenge for students is to figure out how they might go about solving the problem. Students' key first steps will be to think about the information they need to know and how they might go about getting that information.

Discuss

Give each group a chance to present their process and their solutions for the first two questions: How far would you go? How long would it take you? As each group shares, ask the audience to consider whether they find the process convincing and why. Invite the class to ask clarifying questions and offer feedback on the features of the work that were and were not yet convincing.

After all groups have had the chance to share, ask the students to look at how each group's solution is similar to or different from their own group's work. No two groups will have arrived at the same answer. Ask students to discuss with their groups what others tried that was similar to their own work and why they think answers were different. Then discuss as a class:

- What are the sources of the differences?
- How similar are the results? Why?

In this part of the discussion, you'll want students to be able to identify the features of different approaches that might have contributed to similar results (such as a similar process) and those that contributed to differences (such as different initial measurements for a step length).

Explore

Ask students, Where could you go walking 10,000 steps? Students will need access to maps of your area to address this question. Students might elect to start from your school or from their homes, depending on what makes sense in your area. You might also ask them to create a 10,000-step route using a map that includes a scale they can use. Ask students to make a display of their map to share with the rest of the class.

Look-Fors

- **How are students trying to enter the investigation? How are they determining what information they need and how to get it?** This is perhaps the most challenging aspect of this task—and a feature that it shares with authentic real-world problems. The task is not phrased to indicate the steps needed to solve it. You can support students in thinking about how to break this investigation into smaller bites that they can take on, or in imagining a simpler problem, like walking 100 steps, as a way to enter the task. You might ask students to reflect on why they feel stuck or what it is about the task that seems hard, and then help them think of a pathway around that challenge.

- **How are students finding the length of a step?** There are many strategies students might use, from trying to measure a single "typical" step to walking multiple steps and finding the average step length. They may grapple with whether to include the length of the walker's feet or only the distance between them. Because these small measurements will naturally introduce error that gets magnified in a problem like this, encouraging students to think carefully about all small measurements will make a big difference in each group's solutions.

- **How are students selecting and moving between units?** When solving for distance or time, there are multiple reasonable units students might select—yards or miles, meters or kilometers, minutes or hours. But students are likely to make initial measurements in smaller units, such as inches, feet, minutes, and seconds. Probe students' reasoning about how they are choosing what units they think make sense and how they are using unit relationships to move into the units they select. Encourage students to label their calculations with units as they work, to maintain clarity for themselves and others.

Reflect

How did you decide what units to use while you investigated? How did you use unit relationships while you investigated?

BIG IDEA 5

Modeling with Unit Fractions

Many students are confused by fractions, and it is not hard to understand why. When students are introduced to fractions as sets of rules and methods, they become very muddled. When you multiply fractions, you multiply the numerator and the denominator, but when you add fractions, you cannot add the numerators and denominators; instead you have to find common denominators and add the numerators. Division involves another set of rules. Students try to memorize these seemingly nonsensical ideas and often become confused. I have found in my teaching and work with students that the most important idea for students when learning fractions is the idea of a relationship. I teach students that what is special about a fraction is that the numerator relates to the denominator and that we do not know anything about the fraction without knowing what that relationship is. A fraction is big only if the numerator is a large proportion of the denominator, because the numerator and denominator are related. When students are taught rules about how to change the numerator and how to change the denominator, they start to see fractions as separate numbers and lose the critical idea of the relationship. In this big idea and the next, we will encourage students to see fractions as a relationship.

Another reason that students become confused about the meaning of fractions is that they mainly see fractions—often with diagrams—as parts of a whole. Visual representations are imperative for students, but when students only see fractions as part of a pizza, a pie, or a rectangle, they get the idea that a fraction is a piece of a whole. This became very clear in a research study conducted by the Strategies and Errors in Secondary Mathematics Project in London (Kerslake, 1986). The study was conducted many years ago now, but is still among the most important research we have on students learning fractions. A team looked at students' learning of fractions, ratios, decimals, and algebra and the main misconceptions students developed. One of the questions they gave to students in an interview was to plot $\frac{3}{5}$ on a number line, which looked like this:

Not one of the 12- and 13-year-olds plotted the point correctly, even though they all accurately placed $1\frac{1}{5}$. Why would students be more accurate with a mixed number like $1\frac{1}{5}$ than a fraction like $\frac{3}{5}$, with which they are familiar? The students all saw $\frac{3}{5}$ as a piece of something and not a number, and could not think about it being placed on a number line. Some of the students tried to work out $\frac{3}{5}$ of the whole line that was drawn.

I thought this result was very interesting, as it reveals a common problem in the teaching of fractions: students often do not see a fraction as a number. They see a fraction as two numbers and think of it as a piece of one object. When we teach students that a fraction represents one number, they start to see the relationship that the number conveys. From the idea of a relationship, they also more easily see the need for equivalence, which we will come to in our next big idea.

In our Visualize activity, we invite students to see fractions on a number line. This will help students see fractions as a number and not only a piece of something. Students are given the opportunity to make their own measuring unit, which will help them realize that mathematics can be an open and creative activity, not just a set of rules, as many students think. They will use their own unit of measurement to measure objects around the room, and they will use each other's units of measurement and give feedback to each other. The giving of feedback to others is another important mathematical act. Encourage students' creative naming of their units of measurement; they will enjoy giving their units interesting names! This activity gives students an opportunity to consider and use fractions on a line and to see the value of fractions in measurement.

In our Play activity, students will get a lot of experience with unit fractions, seeing the ways a tangram square is made and making their own square using the fractions from the original square. They will then be invited to make different fractions, with some being under 1 and some over, again using tangram pieces. We are asking students to plot on a number line the fractions they make, so that students see that the fractions represent one number. We have invited students to make tangrams so that they experience mathematics as a creative subject, and they also receive opportunities to make choices about the shapes they make. Students should be offered regular opportunities to make choices as they work, as this is part of being mathematical and also supports the brain in working optimally.

Our Investigate activity is an adaptation of one from Picklemath—a lovely collection of investigations. The authors of the investigations on this website particularly value and share unsolved math problems—problems that no one has ever solved but that are completely accessible to schoolchildren. Such problems are very exciting for students of all ages. In this investigation, students will be given the opportunity to think deeply, as the problems are challenging—but the low floor means that all students will understand the problems and know what they need to know to tackle them. If students tell you the problems are hard, tell them that is good: it means their brains are growing! The students will again have an opportunity to use unit fractions and to start to think about equivalence, which is the next of our big ideas.

Jo Boaler

Perplexing Measures

Snapshot

In this activity, students build a number line of fractional values as their own unit of measure. Students will measure objects and use fractions as values on a number line.

Connection to CCSS
4.NF.1
4.NF.2
4.NF.3
4.NF.4

Agenda

Activity	Time	Description/ Prompt	Materials
Launch	5 min	Show your own measuring tape and show students how you measure the length of an object of your choice. When you show students the measuring tape, ask them for suggestions on how to describe the measurement length. Record a few measurements as examples.	Teacher-made measuring tape
Explore	30 min	Students create their own measuring tape, give the unit of measurement a name, and choose three objects in the room to measure and label. Students create a visual display of the items they measured, with descriptive labels showing the measurements.	• Long strips of paper a minimum of two feet long. Each strip should be a different length. We like to use adding-machine tape. • Colored markers. • Objects for the class to measure. • Paper to record and display the measurements of their objects.

Discuss	10 min	Students explore another measurement station and verify the unit of measure that another group has used. Students leave feedback for the group, and another object that they have measured and labeled using that measurement tool. Students share their experience of making their own unit of measurement that has fractions of a unit.	
Extend	20+ min	Given objects and measurements from another group's station, students re-create the measuring tape the group used.	Measuring tape, for each group to cut to length

To the Teacher

This lesson asks students to make their own unit of measure and then classify objects around them. Their unit of measure is created by taking a strip of paper designated as two units long. They begin by folding their 2-unit paper in half over several iterations, labeling the fold lines and then using their measuring tape to identify the lengths of common objects around the classroom.

Activity

Launch

To launch this activity, show students the measuring tape you have made for yourself. To make this measuring tape, use a strip of paper that is between 1 and 2 meters long. We like to use adding-machine tape. To prepare your tape, fold it in half and crease the fold. Label this mark 1 unit. Continue to fold in half and mark the units until you have a measuring tape that is two units long and is broken down into units that represent eighths, quarters, and halves. See Figure 5.1.

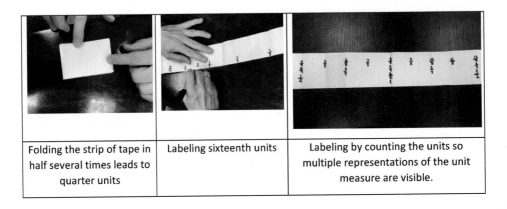

| Folding the strip of tape in half several times leads to quarter units | Labeling sixteenth units | Labeling by counting the units so multiple representations of the unit measure are visible. |

Figure 5.1

In the third box in Figure 5.1, you can see equivalent fractions listed for the units of measure. This is a good practice to show students the meaning of equivalence.

Use a creative name for your unit of measurement. We called our example unit a zoomboogle.

Model measuring items around the room with your measuring tape. In our examples (see Figure 5.2), we measured a tangram shape, a stuffed London black cab and a meter stick.

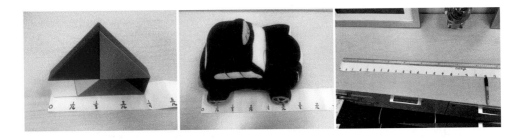

Figure 5.2

You may want to see how your students do at estimating the measure of different objects before you measure and record. Make sure to use the name of your unit of measurement as you measure.

Explore

Provide each pair of students a different-length strip of paper. This strip of paper will represent their measuring unit. Tell the students that their length of paper represents two units. Show them how you have folded it in half several times to break it into smaller units of measure. It's easiest to mark the unit measurements after each fold. Ask students to fold and label their paper so that they can use it to measure objects. After the first fold, students can label 0, 1, and 2 units. After the next fold, they can label half units; after the next fold, quarter units, eighth units, and then sixteenth units. When students are labeling the units, you can have them write all of the equivalent units, or they can write only the equivalent simplified unit.

Because they are all using different-length strips of paper, their unit of measure will be different than all the other groups in class. Each group should name their unit of measure. Figure 5.3 shows a few examples of student measuring devices.

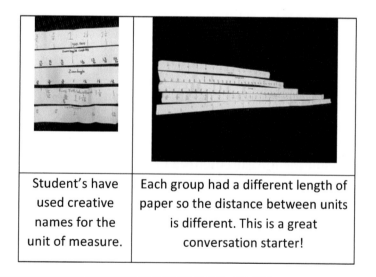

| Student's have used creative names for the unit of measure. | Each group had a different length of paper so the distance between units is different. This is a great conversation starter! |

Figure 5.3

The next part of the task is for each group to choose three different common classroom items to measure. As they measure the items, they should use accurate units and make descriptive statements as to what they are measuring. For example, they may measure the circumference of a ball and the height of a desk. Their labels of measure should be clear so that other students know what has been measured and what dimension of the item has been measured. After students measure their three objects, they should create a display showing the objects and their official measure.

Discuss

After students have created their measurement display, ask other groups to move around the room verifying the measurements using the measuring tape created by the group that made the display. Students can leave feedback notes for the groups as they move around the room. Giving feedback is a nice activity for students to practice. You can extend the activity by asking a visiting group to find a new object and label it using the group's unit of measure. When the groups return to their home stations, they can verify the new items that have been left with measurements.

Then gather students together to discuss the following questions:

- What challenged you in this activity? How did you respond to that challenge?
- We all measured and used the same process to develop our measuring strip. If we measure the same object with two different measuring strips, will the measurements be the same?
- Did the items you measured match your measuring tape exactly? If not, what did you do?

Extend

Ask groups to re-create the measuring tape for one of the other group displays. You will need to hide the measuring tapes the groups used for the displays they made. Give the group verifying the measurements a new strip of paper and ask them to work together to come up with a replica of the measuring tape that was used to measure the items. When the new measuring tape has been made, ask the groups to return to their original station and compare the new measuring tape to the original one they created.

Look-Fors

- **Do students fold their measuring strips with precision? Are they paying attention to equal units?** Students' folds should create equal-size regions in order to support accurate measurements. If students' folds are noticeably unequal, ask questions about whether this matters, when, and why. Press students to be precise and to think about how the units are used together to make larger units. For instance, it should be that $\frac{1}{4}$ twice is the same as $\frac{2}{4}$ or $\frac{1}{2}$.

- **Do students count and label their units accurately?** Students should count using the fractions as units. For instance, support students to count by fourths: $\frac{1}{4}, \frac{2}{4}, \frac{3}{4}, \frac{4}{4}, \frac{5}{4}$, and so on. Notice how students address fractions greater than one. This is another place to attend to equivalence, as these numbers can be written both as improper fractions and mixed numbers.

- **Are students becoming comfortable with using equivalent names for fractions—for example, that $\frac{2}{4}$ is $\frac{1}{2}$?** Ask questions about how one set of units labeled across their measuring tape relates to the other units that have already been labeled. For instance, $\frac{2}{4}$ has a relationship with $\frac{1}{2}$. You might ask, what does it mean that $\frac{2}{4}$ and $\frac{1}{2}$ occupy the same place on the measuring tape?

Reflect

How are fractions useful when measuring an object?

Tangram Designs

Snapshot

In this activity, students use tangrams to build fractions less than, equal to, and greater than a whole in different ways. Students discuss how determining what fraction each piece of the tangram set represents helps them build larger fractions.

Connection to CCSS
4.NF.1
4.NF.3

Agenda

Activity	Time	Description/Prompt	Materials
Launch	10 min	Introduce tangrams and make observations about the shapes. If we define the tangram square as one whole, what other ways can we use the pieces to construct a whole?	Tangram set, arranged in a square
Play	20+ min	Students work in partnerships to determine what fraction of the square each tangram piece represents. Students then use multiple copies of tangram sets to find new ways to make squares the same size as the original tangram square, and display these on a poster.	• Tangram sets, multiple copies per group • Tape or glue • Posters and markers
Discuss	10 min	Discuss the different squares students have created and how the fractions supported them in making squares. Share creative solutions.	Student posters

Play	30 min	Students then use the tangram sets to create different shapes that represent a fraction of their choosing: $\frac{1}{2}$, $\frac{9}{16}$, $\frac{3}{4}$, $\frac{7}{8}$, 1, $1\frac{1}{2}$, or $\frac{7}{4}$ Partnerships create posters to show their solutions.	• Tangram sets, multiple copies per group • Tape or glue • Posters and markers
Discuss	15 min	Discuss how students used the tangram pieces to help them create the different fractions. Students highlight the most creative solutions and discuss why some fractions were more difficult than others to construct with the tangram pieces.	Student posters
Extend	30+ min	Students create their own shape sets by decomposing a square the same size as the tangram set they have been working with throughout the lesson. They then try to use their pieces to construct a fraction of their choosing and investigate what fractions their set is useful for constructing.	• Shape Set Template, multiple copies per group • Tape or glue • Posters and markers

To the Teacher

This activity can continue across multiple days, particularly if you include the extension activity. We encourage you, for as long as students are intrigued and engaged, to follow your students' interest and explore how tangram shapes—and the shape sets students create—can be used to construct larger fractions. For the extension, we have provided a template whose outline is the same size as the tangram square used in the lesson. Inside are dots, arranged like dot paper, so that the square is 8×8. This structure should support students in decomposing the square into fractions that have denominators in the same family as the tangrams: halves, fourths, eighths, sixteenths, and so on. The dots should also help students determine what fraction each shape represents. However, some students may not use this dot structure at all. They might fold their paper and create thirds, fifths, or sixths. Celebrate the creative ways students come up with. Engage students in thinking about how they can prove what fraction each piece represents. Students will discover interesting things about what fractions they can—and cannot—build with these pieces.

Activity

Launch

Launch this task by reminding students of the work they have been doing building fractions with unit fractions. In today's investigation, we are going to continue our work with building, but this time we are going to investigate how we can use a set of shapes called tangrams to think about fractions. Introduce a tangram set by showing the pieces assembled into a square. You can use either manipulatives or the provided template. If your students have not used tangrams before, you might ask them to make some observations about the pieces and tell them that the group is a set of tangrams. Students should notice the different types of shapes and their different sizes. They might also notice how they relate to each other or the whole—for instance, that each large triangle is $\frac{1}{4}$ of the square or that the two smallest triangles can be put together to make the small square.

The seven tangram pieces can be arranged in a particular square. In today's activity, we are going to be using sets of tangrams to investigate how the pieces might be used in different ways to create other squares that are the same size. To help us think about this, we will also be asking what fraction of the whole square each piece is.

Play

Working in pairs, ask students to determine the following:

- What fraction of the square is each piece?
- How can these pieces be used to make new squares that are the same size as the original tangram square?
- How many different squares can you create?

Students should use multiple copies of the tangram squares provided to work on these questions. Ask students to use one tangram square to record the fraction each piece represents and to show on the square their evidence for the fraction names they give to each piece.

Students can then cut out multiple sets of tangrams to uses as pieces for constructing new squares. It is an important constraint of the problem that the squares should be the same size as the original tangram square. If you have tangram manipulatives, students can use these to try to build new squares, though keep in mind they will be the same size as the tangram square made by your manipulatives rather than the one on our sheet. When students identify a solution, invite them to tape or glue the paper pieces to a poster as a record. Students should also label each piece with the fraction it represents.

Encourage students to find as many possibilities as they can. You might ask students how they can modify solutions they have already found to create new solutions. You might also ask how the fractions can help them find new solutions.

Discuss

Ask students to display their posters so that all students can see the different solutions the class generated. Give students a moment to look over these solutions, then ask:

- What do you notice?
- How did you go about generating squares? What strategies did you develop?
- How did the fractions help you build the squares?
- How did you modify your solutions to create new squares? (Students might have used equivalence to swap pieces out. Be sure to highlight this kind of thinking.)
- What was the most creative or interesting square you made? Why? What is the most creative or interesting square someone else made? Why?

Play

The square we've been working with is our whole, or 1. In this next exploration, invite students to choose a fraction from the list here and ask them to create as many different ways to represent that fraction with the tangram shapes as possible:

$$\frac{1}{2} \qquad \frac{9}{16} \qquad \frac{3}{4} \qquad \frac{7}{8} \qquad 1 \qquad 1\frac{1}{2} \qquad \frac{7}{4}$$

Again, students can cut out the tangram shapes from the template provided and glue or tape these down on a poster for their fraction. Students should also label the fractions represented by each piece. Students can create any shape—not just squares—that uses pieces to represent the fraction they chose.

Encourage students to try building shapes for more than one fraction and to try to build more than one shape for each fraction. By trying to build in multiple ways, they will learn more about how to use the unit fractions flexibly and to work with equivalence between the pieces.

Discuss

Gather students for a discussion of the following questions:

- What strategies did you use in making your shapes so that they matched the fraction you chose?
- How did you use the fraction values of each piece to help you?
- What was the most creative shape you made? Why?
- If you built more than one fraction, what fractions were easier or harder to create shapes for? Why?

Extend

Students have been working with a classic set of tangrams, seven shapes decomposed from a square. Creating a shape set like tangrams, one that is flexible and contains many relationships, is difficult. In this extension, challenge students to create their own set of shapes by decomposing a square into some number of smaller shapes. We have provided a square template on dot paper to support students in thinking about how to decompose a square into a set of pieces that might be useful for building. Provide groups with this template (they will need multiple copies) and ask them to decompose it into a set of shapes and give a fraction name to each shape. This is an important constraint in this task: the shapes they create should be those that they know how to name with a fraction. Then ask students to repeat the previous exploration with their new pieces: choose a fraction (from the list or their own), cut out shapes, and create a new shape that matches the fraction they chose.

You may want to ask students to share their new shape sets and the ways they represented fractions with them. Students might find that their pieces cannot be readily used to build some of the fractions we suggested. This presents an interesting opportunity to probe why only some fractions can be used to build another. For instance, $\frac{1}{8}$ pieces can be used to build $\frac{1}{2}$, but $\frac{1}{3}$ pieces cannot.

Alternatively, you could use the new shape sets students create to provide additional pieces for the entire class to use in constructing shapes that represent fractions. This could extend the previous exploration into another day of work as students find new ways to build fractions like $1\frac{1}{2}$ or $\frac{7}{4}$.

Look-Fors

- **Are students able to accurately determine what fraction each tangram piece represents?** Students might name each piece as a unit fraction: $\frac{1}{4}$,

$\frac{1}{8}$, and $\frac{1}{16}$. Or students might think in terms of sixteenths to name the pieces: $\frac{4}{16}$, $\frac{2}{16}$, and $\frac{1}{16}$. It will be useful for students to think about which pieces can be used to make others in determining their fractional value. You might also prompt students to consider what the square might look like if it were constructed out of only one kind of piece. In this way, some students might make squares to find the fractional values, rather than using the fractional values to create squares.

- **How are students deciding what pieces to use in making their shapes?** When building squares, students can use the square as a tool for reasoning, much as they would with a jigsaw puzzle. They might ask themselves what shapes would fit, reasoning spatially. As students move on to making shapes other than squares and fractions other than one whole, they will think more about the fractions they are composing than the shape they are composing.

- **How are students modifying one solution to create a new solution?** Once students have created one square (or a target fraction), they can modify their solution by substituting equivalent pieces. For example, the parallelogram could be exchanged for two small triangles without changing the overall shape created (or the fraction it represents). This is a useful strategy for generating multiple solutions, and it also encourages thinking about equivalence.

Reflect

What makes a fraction easier or harder to build? Share some examples to support your thinking.

Tangram Set

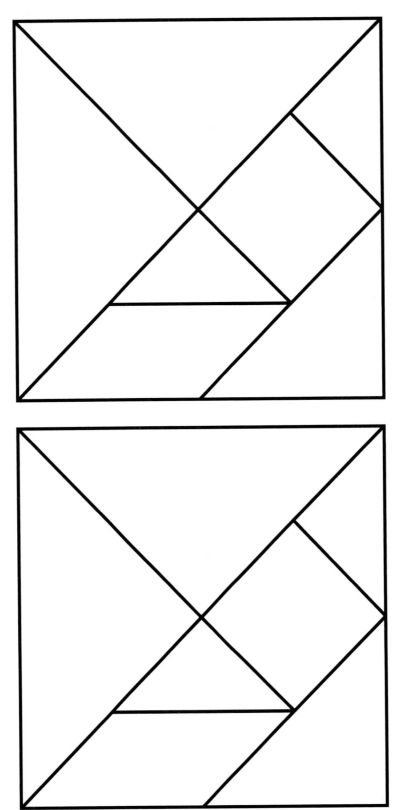

Shape Set Template

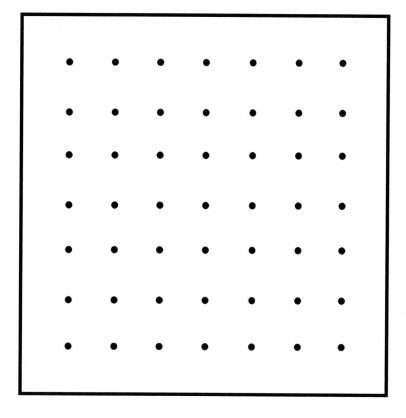

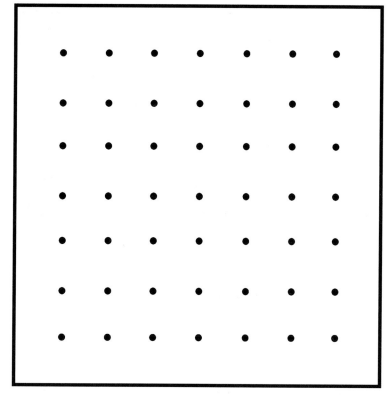

Pixeled Fractions

Snapshot

In this investigation, students work on puzzles that relate fractions and area. Students look for unit fractions inside a grid where the fractional parts are shaded squares of a picture. They will form rectangles to break the picture into smaller pieces where the shaded squares represent the unit fractions they are looking for.

Connection to CCSS
4.NF.1
4.NF.2
4.NF.3
4.NF.4

Agenda

Activity	Time	Description/ Prompt	Materials
Launch	10 min	Display the puzzle, "What Animal Am I?" Ask students to decide what animal the picture represents. Ask them to begin trying to solve the puzzle in small groups. Before students finish, ask them to volunteer the methods they are using to solve the puzzle.	"What Animal Am I?" to display and one copy per group of students
Explore	20 min	Give each group of students copies of the pixeled fraction puzzles. Ask them to work on a puzzle and move on when they are ready for a different puzzle. When a group has a solution to a puzzle, ask them to prepare a proof showing how they know their answer is correct.	• Puzzles, copied for groups: ○ Is This a Tree? ○ What Could This Be? ○ Dog or Cat? ○ What Is This? • Rulers

Discuss	10+ min	As a class, discuss the strategies that students used. Share the solutions and the proofs that students prepared. Discuss how they used unit fractions and other equivalent fractions.	
Extend	20+ min	Give students an empty grid or graph paper so that they can create their own fraction puzzle.	• Grid paper (see appendix) or a copy of the Make Your Own Fraction Puzzle! • Markers • Ruler • Optional: page protectors and dry erase markers

To the Teacher

This activity has several puzzles that give students a chance to explore fractions and area in a visual display. Once students have completed a few puzzles, they will be ready to create their own visual fraction puzzles.

Activity

Launch

Display the "What Animal Am I?" puzzle. Ask students to decide what animal they think this could be. Come to a class agreement on the type of animal and then proceed to the puzzle as a class. The goal isn't to finish the puzzle together but to discuss the puzzle and problem-solve together. Give students an opportunity to discuss ideas and strategy in small groups and then ask for volunteers to share with the class. The goal is to have students share before anyone has had a chance to solve the puzzle. If a solution is posed, ask the group to prove their solution works.

Explore

Ask students to work on the different pixeled fraction puzzles in small groups. Let them know that they can work on any of the puzzles. If they get stuck on one, they can always move on to another puzzle. There is no need to complete the puzzles in any order. Even mathematicians take breaks from challenging work.

When students solve a puzzle, ask them to make a proof showing that their solution is accurate. Is there only one way to solve the puzzle?

Discuss

Gather students together to discuss the following questions:

- What strategies did you use to solve the puzzle?
- Did your strategies change as you solved more puzzles?
- Were some puzzles more challenging? Why?
- What do you need to do to prove you have a solution?

Extend

Ask students to create their own visual fraction puzzle. A blank grid is included, but students do not need to restrict themselves to that space. They can use a grid of any size they choose. After students create puzzles, we encourage you to photocopy these puzzles for students to swap, or place the puzzles inside a page protector for students to use a dry erase marker to solve.

Look-Fors

- **What strategies are students using to solve the puzzles?** Are they drawing random lines and rectangles and then counting, or are they counting before trying to draw the lines and rectangles? Students may well guess at the beginning; it is a strategy that makes a lot of sense to start with. However, as students test their guesses, they should learn what fractions are created and think about how they might modify their partitions to get closer to the fractions they are targeting. Ask, What could you do to this section to get closer to $\frac{1}{2}$ (or $\frac{1}{3}$ or whatever fraction they are looking for)? Students will also need to think about how their modifications to one rectangle impact the others.

- **Are students using equivalent representations for the unit fractions in their problem solving?** Do students find the area of a rectangle and translate that into an equivalent fraction that is equal to the unit fraction they are trying to find? For example, this rectangle has sides of 6 and 4, so the area is 24. That means $\frac{12}{24}$ squares should be shaded if $\frac{1}{2}$ of the rectangle is to be shaded. Moving between the fraction, equivalent fractions, and the number of squares is useful for solving these puzzles.

Reflect

What strategies did you find helpful when solving these fraction puzzles?

Reference

Kerslake, D. (1986). *Fractions: Children's strategies and errors. A report of the Strategies and Errors in Secondary Mathematics Project.* Windsor. England: NFER-Nelson.

What Animal Am I?

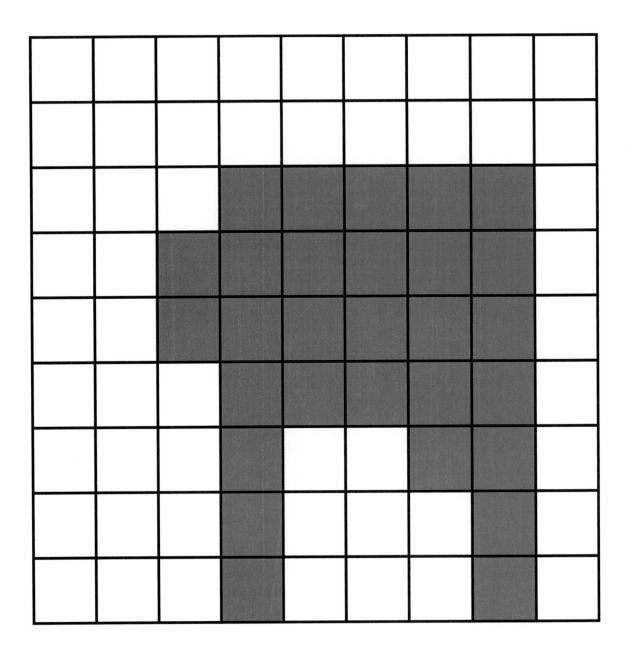

Draw two straight lines that break the large square into four smaller rectangles. Two rectangles are $\frac{1}{3}$ shaded, one is $\frac{1}{2}$ shaded, and one is $\frac{1}{5}$ shaded.

Is This a Tree?

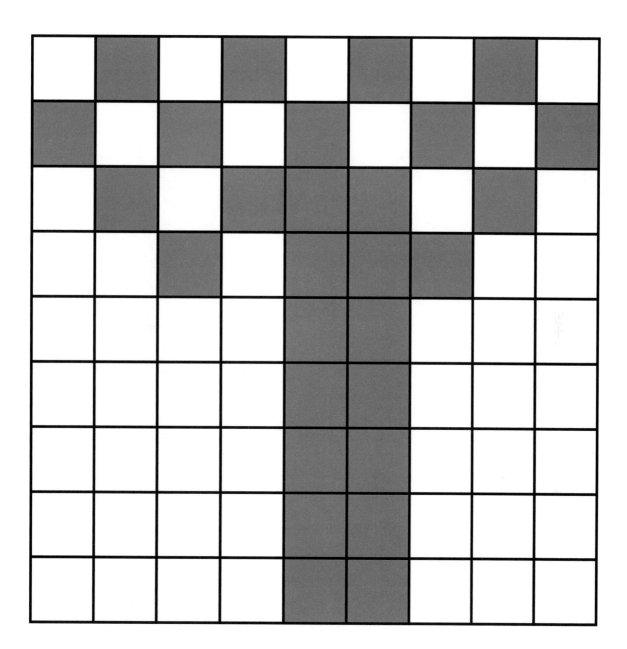

Draw three rectangles so that one is $\frac{1}{4}$ shaded, one is $\frac{1}{5}$ shaded, and the other is $\frac{1}{2}$ shaded.

What Could This Be?

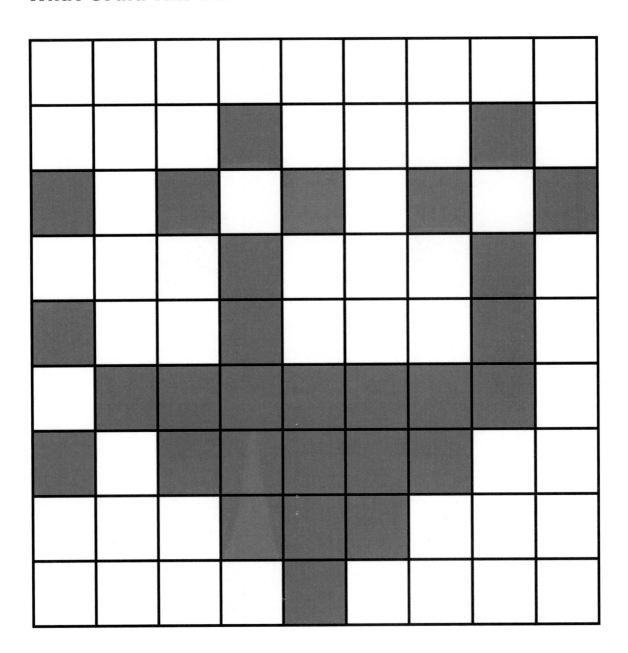

Draw three rectangles so that one is $\frac{1}{3}$ shaded, one is $\frac{1}{2}$ shaded, and the other is $\frac{1}{4}$ shaded.

Dog or Cat?

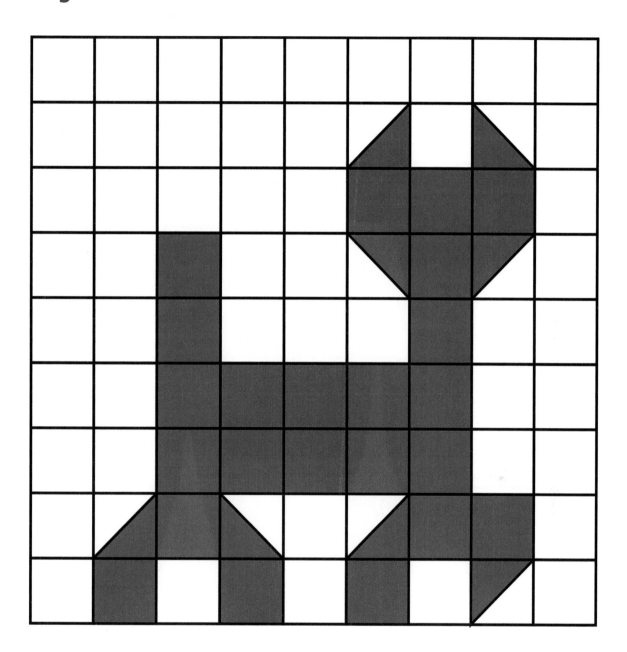

Draw one straight line that divides the large square into two smaller rectangles. One rectangle is $\frac{1}{2}$ shaded, and the other is $\frac{1}{5}$ shaded.

What Is This?

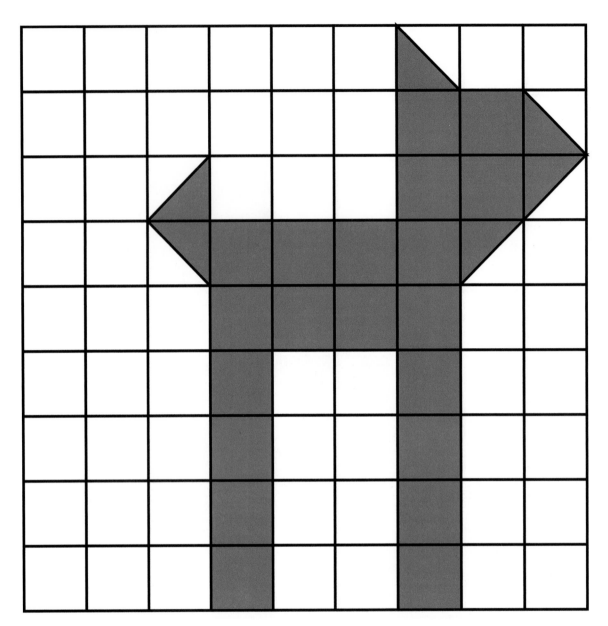

Draw two straight lines that break the large square into four smaller rectangles. One rectangle is $\frac{1}{2}$ shaded, one is $\frac{1}{4}$ shaded, and two are $\frac{1}{5}$ shaded.

Make Your Own Fraction Puzzle!

Exploring Fraction Equivalence

In the research on fraction understanding conducted by the Strategies and Errors in Secondary Mathematics Project in London, students were given different fraction questions to solve. When the researchers looked across all of the results, collected from over 800 students, they concluded that students knew how to use different methods with fractions, but they made mistakes because they lacked an understanding of what a fraction really was, beyond a part of a whole. I talked about this in the introduction to Big Idea 5, and mentioned the helpfulness of seeing fractions on a number line. I also discussed the importance of students seeing fractions as a relationship—one number—that comes from the way that the numerator and denominator relate to each other. When students understand fractions as a relationship, they are better able to understand equivalence, something they need when adding or subtracting fractions.

Equivalence is a key idea in working with fractions and one that underlies the methods of addition, ordering, and subtraction. Equivalence draws on the idea of a relationship, as it involves thinking about the numerator and denominator of a fraction together. One of the results of the London study of 800 students (Kerslake, 1986) showed the common error students make when thinking about fraction addition. When students were asked to add $\frac{1}{3}$ and $\frac{1}{4}$, 29% of 13-year-olds, 22% of 14-year-olds and 20% of 15-year-olds gave the answer $\frac{2}{7}$. When students give this answer, they are thinking of the numerators as two numbers they can add and the dominators as two numbers they can add; they are not thinking of each fraction as one number. Fundamentally, students should understand that they cannot add quarters and thirds without changing them into equivalent fractions.

In our Visualize activity, students are given an opportunity to deepen their understanding of a common denominator with the key idea that fractions are made up of equal-size pieces. A common misconception in fraction understanding is thinking that fractions need to be not only the same size but also the same shape. This is not the case, and some of the examples in our Visualize activity show equal fractions that are different shapes. It will be good to point this idea out to students. We have provided real artwork to integrate fractions with art and to give students the opportunity to work with color.

In our Play activity, students are given the opportunity to make their own fractions in a brownie pan. We start the activity with an open question for students to explore. Students again get to see that fractions can be the same size but different shapes. We ask the students: "How many different ways can you color the brownie pan?" as this gives students choice—which is important—and an opportunity to investigate different possibilities with their peers.

In our Investigate activity, students are asked to create their own rectangles and to look for patterns in the tables of equivalent fractions that are produced in the whole-class discussion. In the creation of different rectangles that satisfy certain constraints, students are again asked both to draw visual arrays and to write with numbers, encouraging the use of different brain pathways and brain connections. This activity includes opportunity for choices to be made as there are many possible solutions, and for students to have good conversations about fraction equivalence when they have made their different rectangles.

Jo Boaler

Painting Pieces

Snapshot

Students begin to build understanding of the need for equal-size pieces—a common denominator—by exploring the colors used in a geometric painting. Students try to give fractional names to the colored regions and grapple with the idea of unequal areas.

Connection to CCSS
4.NF.1
4.NF.2

Agenda

Activity	Time	Description/Prompt	Materials
Launch	5 min	Introduce students to examples of geometric art. Pose the task of figuring out the fraction of each color in the painting. After finding the fraction area of each color, students will order the fraction areas.	• Examples of geometric art • Painting Pieces pages, to show students
Explore	30 min	Partners work to develop strategies for finding the fraction each color represents in different paintings.	Painting Pieces pages, copied for partners to choose from. Partners may try more than one.
Discuss	15 min	Discuss strategies that students developed and connect their thinking to the central idea that a common unit or piece size was needed across the colors.	Examples of students' strategies
Extend	20+ min	Students generate their own design that matches the color fractions they found in one of the paintings.	• Dot paper (see appendix), multiple sheets per partnership • Colors (markers, crayons, or colored pencils)

To the Teacher

Color is an important part of this activity, but we know that color copying is not always possible. We're providing both color and gray-scale examples of each painting. If students use the gray-scale painting to find the fractions, they will likely find the extension more interesting if they can substitute colors for the grays. For instance, students could substitute red for black, green for light gray, yellow for dark gray, and orange for white. This will make their own paintings more interesting for them to construct and feel proud of.

Activity

Launch

Launch the lesson by sharing with your students some examples of geometric art-work. You might want to find some examples from around your school, museum websites, or art books from the library to show, or you can show the artwork we have provided. Figure 6.1 shows one example students will work with today. The artists who made these paintings use color and shapes to create interesting patterns and feelings. The artist might use one color a lot and a different color only a little. But how much of each color is there? Tell students that today we are going to look at some geometric paintings like the ones you've shown and try to figure out what fraction of the painting each color represents. Show students the paintings as you explain the task.

Figure 6.1
Inspired by *Double Concentric: Scramble,* by Frank Stella, 1971.

Explore

Allow each group or partnership to choose one of the Painting Pieces pages to start their exploration. Students should try to develop a strategy for finding the fraction of the painting that each color represents. Students should record their strategies and evidence on the Painting Pieces pages, showing both the fractions they found and how they found them. If partners finish one painting, they can choose another to try. Encourage students to challenge themselves with paintings they might not be certain how to tackle. Ask students to write number sentences showing the fraction relationships of the different colored areas for each painting. For the example in Figure 6.1, a student might write:

$$\text{Blue area} > \text{purple area, because } \frac{32}{100} > \frac{16}{100} \text{ or } \frac{8}{25} > \frac{4}{25}$$

$$\text{Yellow area} = \text{red area, because } \frac{2}{100} = \frac{2}{100} \text{ or } \frac{1}{50} = \frac{1}{50}$$

Discuss

Gather students together to discuss the following questions:

- What strategies did you and your partner come up with to find the fraction each color represented?
- Did different paintings require different strategies? Or could you use the same strategy on all the paintings? Why?

Examine some of the paintings, particularly one that many students chose and any one that posed challenges for students. Ask:

- What fraction of the painting does each color represent? How do you know?
- Did anyone find a different fraction name for the same region?
- Can more than one answer be correct? Why or why not?
- Which colors were the most challenging to figure out? Why? What did (or could) you do to deal with this challenge?

Extend

Once you have established fraction values for colors on one or more paintings, students can create their own designs. Challenge students to create a painting with color fractions that match one of the paintings they explored. They should think creatively about how to use the space so that their painting looks different while still using the same color fractions. Students can create multiple paintings to explore the different ways they might represent the fractions. Students should label their paintings with the fractions used by each color.

Note that this task is more challenging than identifying the fractions in the existing paintings, and students might struggle to develop a strategy that works. Their paintings do not need to be any particular size, and you can encourage them to explore the dimensions they want to work with to create the fractions they want to match.

We encourage you to display the different paintings students create, perhaps clustered around a copy of the paintings they are emulating. This can allow others to see how the balance of colors is the same even when the shapes are different.

Look-Fors

- **Are students noticing that the regions for each color are different sizes?** Some students may simply see four colors, say, in four regions and conclude that each is one-fourth. Challenge these conclusions by asking how a small region and a large region can both be the same fraction.

- **How are students attempting to decompose the space to find fractions?** All the paintings can be decomposed into equal-size shapes, but not all students will choose the same shapes or sizes. Notice whether students are using the smallest shapes as clues to help them decompose. If not, ask what they plan to do with that piece.

- **Are students giving different fraction names to the same regions?** This is a critical opportunity to make connections to equivalence. If students use different-size pieces to decompose the figure, they will naturally use different denominators. In the discussion, be sure to put these equivalent forms front and center and ask questions about how they can both be true.

Reflect

How did decomposing the paintings help you find the fraction each color represented?

Painting Pieces

Inspired by *Red, Yellow, Blue*, by Ellsworth Kelly, 1963.

- Find the area of each color in the picture below.

- Write each area as a fraction.

- Write statements stating the fraction equivalence and order using the symbols <, >, and =.

Painting Pieces

Inspired by *Red, Yellow, Blue*, by Ellsworth Kelly, 1963.

- Find the area of each color in the picture below.

- Write each area as a fraction.

- Write statements stating the fraction equivalence and order using the symbols <, >, and =.

Painting Pieces

Inspired by *Double Concentric: Scramble,* by Frank Stella, 1971.

- Find the area of each color in the picture below.

- Write each area as a fraction.

- Write statements stating the fraction equivalence and order using the symbols <, >, and =.

Painting Pieces

Inspired by *Double Concentric: Scramble,* by Frank Stella, 1971.

- Find the area of each color in the picture below.

- Write each area as a fraction.

- Write statements stating the fraction equivalence and order using the symbols <, >, and =.

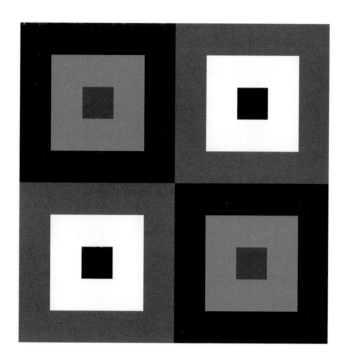

Painting Pieces

Inspired by *Composition II,* by Piet Mondrian, 1921.

- Find the area of each color in the picture below.

- Write each area as a fraction.

- Write statements stating the fraction equivalence and order using the symbols <, >, and =.

Painting Pieces

Inspired by *Composition II,* by Piet Mondrian, 1921.

- Find the area of each color in the picture below.

- Write each area as a fraction.

- Write statements stating the fraction equivalence and order using the symbols <, >, and =.

Painting Pieces

Jen's Triangles

- Find the area of each color in the picture below.

- Write each area as a fraction.

- Write statements stating the fraction equivalence and order using the symbols <, >, and =.

Color-Coding Fractions

Snapshot

In this activity, students color-code different patterns with an assortment of shapes. The goal is for students to understand that fraction models are not limited to circles and squares.

Connection to CCSS
4.NF.1
4.NF.3

Agenda

Activity	Time	Description/Prompt	Materials
Launch	10 min	Show students the brownie pan diagram and ask them if the brownies are equally shared among Sam and his three friends. Discuss the fraction each friend will get and how students see these fractions in the pan.	Brownie Pan Diagram, to display
Play	30 min	Students play with how to equally share brownies among 8, 6, and 12 friends. Students find multiple ways to color-code the brownie pans to show equal shares and multiple fraction names for these shares.	• Brownie Pan Challenge sheets, one of each sheet for each student • Colors • Optional: colored tiles
Discuss	15+ min	Discuss what ways students found to share the brownies, color-code the pans, and name the fraction each friend gets.	• Blank Brownie Pan Challenge sheets, to record student thinking • Colors
Extend	15 min	Ask students to design a brownie pan, then write and explore their own questions.	• Grid paper (see appendix) • Colors

To the Teacher

The goal of this activity is to provide students opportunities to explore fraction relationships with shapes other than circles and rectangles. Students should understand that fraction relationships can be any shape when the shapes are all equal in area.

BIG IDEA 6: EXPLORING FRACTION EQUIVALENCE

Activity

Launch

Show students the brownie pan diagram (Figure 6.2). Ask them if the brownies are equally shared among Sam and his three friends. Pose the problem in this way, as there may be some misunderstandings that will lead to a good conversation. Ask students to determine how many brownies each person will get. If you word it this way, some students will most likely divide the pan among four individuals and others will divide it among three. The beauty in this activity is the flexibility of 24. Both will come up with a whole-number answer. Collect possible answers as if you are doing a number talk. When all numbers are collected, if there are differences in interpretation, come to agreement about how many people are sharing.

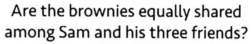

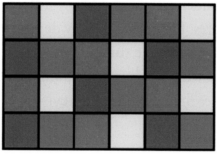

Figure 6.2

Then ask students, How could we name what fraction of the pan each friend will get? Again, take different answers and ask students to discuss how they saw these fraction in the pan. Some students might answer $\frac{1}{4}$ simply because four friends are sharing one whole. Others might see the colors repeating horizontally, every fourth square. Still other students might notice the square of four colors repeated six times. See Figure 6.3 for examples. Others will answer $\frac{6}{24}$ by counting. We encourage you to mark up the example to show how students are seeing the fractions and how the fractions students see are equivalent.

Pose the question, How might you color-code the pan to be shared equally by 8 friends, 6 friends, and 12 friends?

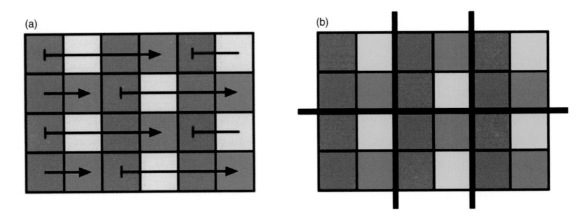

(a)   (b)

Figure 6.3

Play

Ask students to work with a partner to design ways to equally share the brownie pans on the Brownie Pan Challenge sheets among 8 friends, 6 friends, and 12 friends, respectively. Ask students to find as many different ways as they can to color the pans to show equal shares. For each pan they design, students label the fraction of the pan each friend gets. Encourage students to come up with multiple fraction labels, as they did in the launch with $\frac{1}{4}$ and $\frac{6}{24}$. Some students might want to plan their pans using colored tiles first, which make revision easier. Provide these as an option.

Discuss

Gather students together with their different brownie pans. You may want to have a set of blank brownie pans to record their thinking on a document camera. Discuss the following questions:

- How did you share the brownies among eight friends? What fraction of the pan will each friend get? What different ways did you find to color-code the pan to show the equal shares?
- How did you share the brownies among six friends? What fraction of the pan will each friend get? What different ways did you find to color-code the pan to show the equal shares?
- How did you share the brownies among twelve friends? What fraction of the pan will each friend get? What different ways did you find to color-code the pan to show the equal shares?
- How do our different brownie pans help us to see equivalent fractions?

Extend

- Ask students to use grid paper (see appendix) to design their own brownie pan shape.
- How many friends will share?
- How many different ways can you color your brownie pan to show possible solutions?
- What fraction of the pan will each friend get?
- Will there be any leftovers? How will the friends handle the leftovers?

Students can make multiple puzzles and share their findings with the class. You could also ask students to design puzzles to swap with other groups after they have tried the puzzles themselves.

Look-Fors

- **Are students partitioning the pans equally?** Color coding allows students to partition in many ways, which can also lead to organizational and counting challenges. Students may benefit from using colored tiles to rearrange and reorganize the pan while maintaining the number of squares of each color.
- **How are students seeing and naming the fractions?** Some students may simply do as they have in third grade and count the parts—for example, 6 brownies out of 24 brownies in the pan. The question that students need to contend with is why and how this is the same as $\frac{1}{4}$. Push students to justify the fraction names they are giving to each portion and to look for new ways to name those portions.

Reflect

What are the most important things to remember when working with equivalent fractions?

Brownie Pan Diagram

Sam has a pan of brownies that has been cut into equal-size pieces. Sam wants to share the brownies with three of his friends. Have the brownies been shared equally?

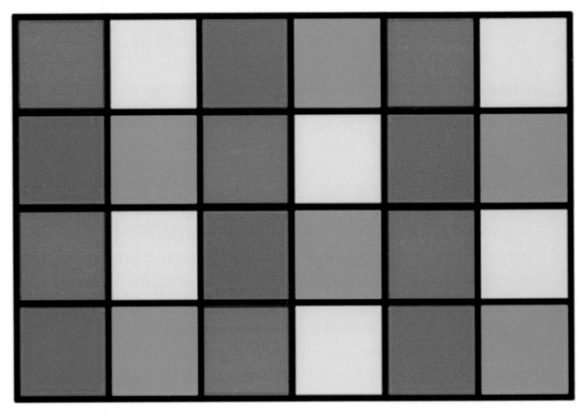

Brownie Pan Challenge

How can the brownies be shared equally by **8 friends**?

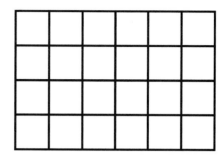
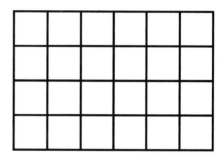
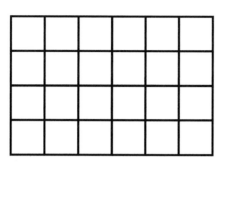
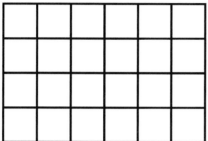
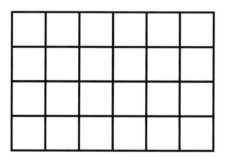
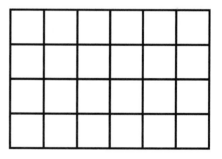

BIG IDEA 6: EXPLORING FRACTION EQUIVALENCE

Brownie Pan Challenge

How can the brownies be shared equally by **6 friends**?

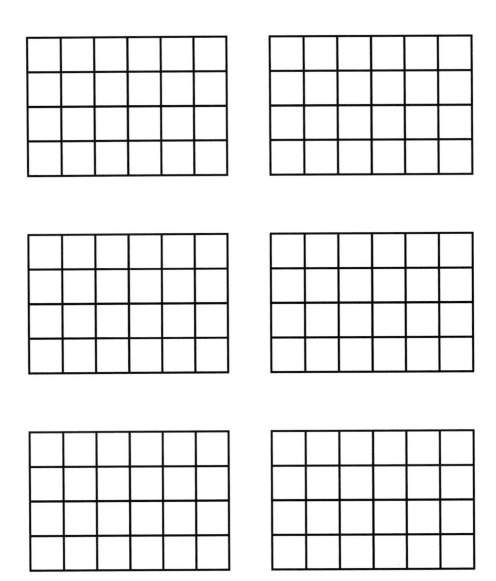

Brownie Pan Challenge

How can the brownies be shared equally by **12 friends**?

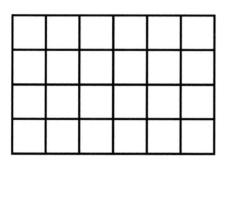
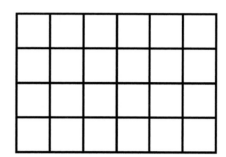

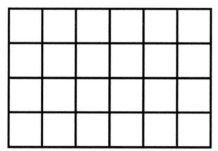
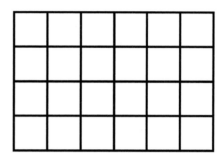

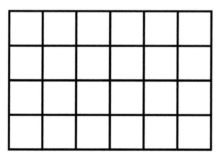
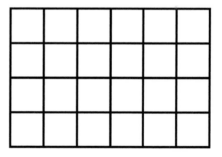

Brownie Pan Challenge

How many brownies are in the pan? If the pan of brownies has been shared equally, how many friends has this pan of brownies been shared with? What fraction of the brownies did each friend get?

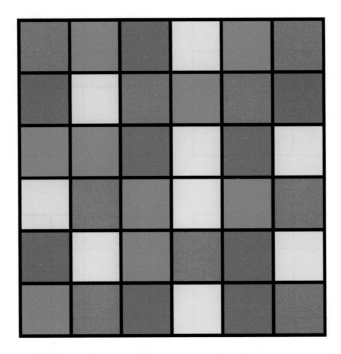

Make your own brownie pan challenge! You can use this pan or make up one of your own!

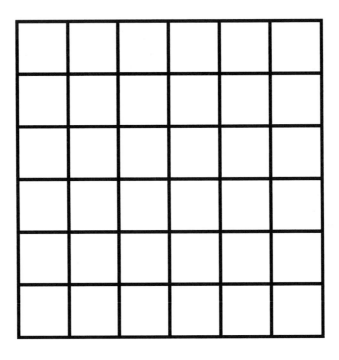

Tiling Rectangles

Snapshot

Students investigate fraction puzzles trying to create rectangles with different proportions of colors. Their goal is to make the smallest rectangle that can satisfy the fraction parameters of the puzzles. The class works together to look for patterns that will help them find rectangles for any set of fractions—a common denominator.

Connection to CCSS
4.NF.1
4.NF.2

Agenda

Activity	Time	Description/Prompt	Materials
Launch	10 min	Remind students of the work they did in the Painting Pieces visual activity, figuring out what fraction of a painting each color represented. Introduce the idea of using tiles to create rectangles with different fractions of colors by trying one together.	• Examples from the Painting Pieces task (see Visualize activity) • Colored tiles
Explore	30+ min	Students work with a partner or in small groups to investigate a series of puzzles, where three colors represent different fractions of a rectangle. Students work together to figure out what size rectangles they can make using colored tiles that match each puzzle.	• Colored tiles, collection of 100 per group • Colored pens or pencils • Tiling Rectangles task sheets, multiple copies per group
Discuss	15 min	The class pools the rectangles they have made in a chart that shows the different areas of the rectangles students made for each puzzle. Use this chart to look for patterns around equivalence and common denominators.	• Student work posted • Chart paper and markers

To the Teacher

The exploration time needed for this investigation will depend on how quickly students see the patterns. You may find that it makes sense to do some sharing at the end of the first day, collecting the rectangles students have made on the class chart, but not hold a full discussion until students have had another day to work and find patterns.

Activity

Launch

Launch this investigation by revisiting the paintings students explored in Painting Pieces, the Visualize activity in this big idea. You might show some of the paintings or some of the students' own work. In that activity, students figured out what fraction of the painting each color represented. In today's investigation, students will be making rectangles like those paintings, where different colors are used and each color represents a fraction of the rectangles. Let's imagine I want to make a rectangle where $\frac{1}{3}$ of the rectangle is blue, $\frac{1}{3}$ is red, and $\frac{1}{3}$ is yellow. What rectangles could I make? We can use colored tiles to make a rectangle. Ask students to turn and talk to a neighbor about ideas for how we could use colored tiles to make a rectangle that is $\frac{1}{3}$ blue, $\frac{1}{3}$ red, and $\frac{1}{3}$ yellow.

Collect some ideas from students and record them for everyone to see. Students might come up with a rectangle that has one tile of each color, two tiles of each color, and so on. Ask students, What is the area of each of these rectangles? What fraction name could we give to each color in these rectangles? Label each one with the area and fractions for each color. Fraction labels will include $\frac{1}{3}$ but also $\frac{2}{6}$ or $\frac{3}{9}$, depending on the rectangle created. Use this as an opportunity to show students how to record, color-code, and label their work.

Tell students that this is what they will be investigating today. We have several puzzles like this where three colors are used to create a rectangle. We know what fraction each color represents, and we want to figure out what size rectangles we can make with these fractions.

Explore

Working in pairs or small groups, students should investigate the puzzles on the Tiling Rectangles task sheets. We recommend that students have access to tiles to physically create their rectangles and explore flexibly what size rectangles can be made. For each rectangle students find that represents the fractions, students should record, label, and color-code it on grid paper (see appendix). Then students should ask, Can we make one that is a different size? Encourage students to make a few different-size rectangles for a puzzle before moving on to a new puzzle. Working on the same puzzle more than once will help students see patterns. For instance, creating and looking across the solutions in Figure 6.4, students might notice that when the blue region is doubled, all other regions are doubled, too.

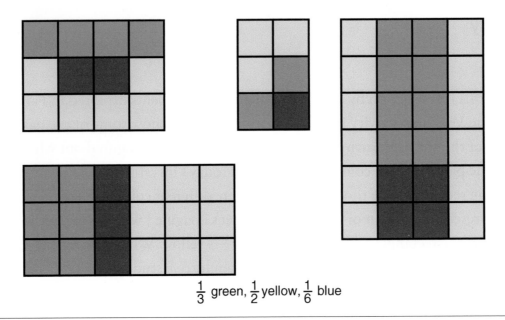

$\frac{1}{3}$ green, $\frac{1}{2}$ yellow, $\frac{1}{6}$ blue

Figure 6.4

For the two final puzzles, the third color does not have a fraction indicated. This color simply makes up the rest of the rectangle. Students should try to make rectangles and figure out what fraction the third color represents. These can be given as an extension or additional challenge.

Discuss

On a chart, create a table with one row for each puzzle students worked on and a column to record the sizes (areas) of the different rectangles students found, such as the one shown in Figure 6.5. Show an example. Tell students that you are going to be

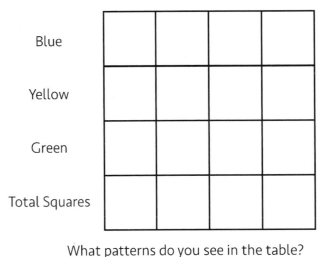

What patterns do you see in the table?

Figure 6.5   Fractional Rectangles Recording Chart

collecting data from the whole class to find patterns. For each puzzle, ask students to share what size rectangles they made. Record these areas in the class table. You may also want to have students post their solutions to each puzzle in a museum of rectangles clustered by puzzle (for example, $\frac{1}{3}$ green, $\frac{1}{2}$ yellow, $\frac{1}{6}$ blue).

Ask the class to look at the results, and discuss the following questions:

- What patterns do you notice? (Note patterns on the chart.)
- If we wanted to predict what rectangles could be made from a set of fractions, how could we do it just by looking at the numbers?

You may want to challenge students to predict the rectangle sizes possible for a set of fractions they have not seen, like $\frac{1}{35}$ red, $\frac{1}{10}$ blue, and $\frac{1}{14}$ yellow. You could then send students back to test their theory by trying to make rectangles using their prediction.

- If we wanted to use our rectangles to decide which fraction in the set was biggest or smallest, how could we do it?

Be sure students notice that creating fractions with a common denominator makes comparison easy. In the case of these rectangles, the common denominator is the rectangle's area. If students have not yet learned this term, take advantage of this opportunity to introduce it when students discuss how the rectangles—and the fractions in them—help them to compare. The patterns they notice in the table of fractions and rectangle sizes are patterns that can help them find a common denominator for any set of fractions.

Look-Fors

- **Are students thinking about the whole and the pieces?** Students may try to build each color separately without thinking about how it relates to the whole rectangle. You may want to ask specifically about the whole to help make the connections: How big is your rectangle? How will you show this fraction in that rectangle?
- **How are students grappling with the different denominators?** These puzzles are not as difficult when the fractions share a denominator, as they do in the example in the launch. But with different denominators, students will need to think across the denominators to try different rectangles, test the colors, and revise.

- **Are students connecting the rectangles they have made for a given puzzle?** You may want to encourage students who have found a solution to a puzzle and ask, How could I revise this rectangle to make a new one that matches the puzzle? We want to create opportunities for students to see that if they doubled (or tripled or halved) the area of each color, a new rectangle could be made.

Reflect

How can you find a common denominator for any set of fractions?

Reference

Kerslake, D. (1986). *Fractions: Children's strategies and errors. A report of the Strategies and Errors in Secondary Mathematics Project.* Windsor, England: NFER-Nelson.

Tiling Rectangles

How many different rectangles can you make that are

$\frac{1}{3}$ green $\frac{1}{2}$ yellow and $\frac{1}{6}$ blue?

Draw each rectangle you find. Label the area and fraction names for each color in the rectangles.

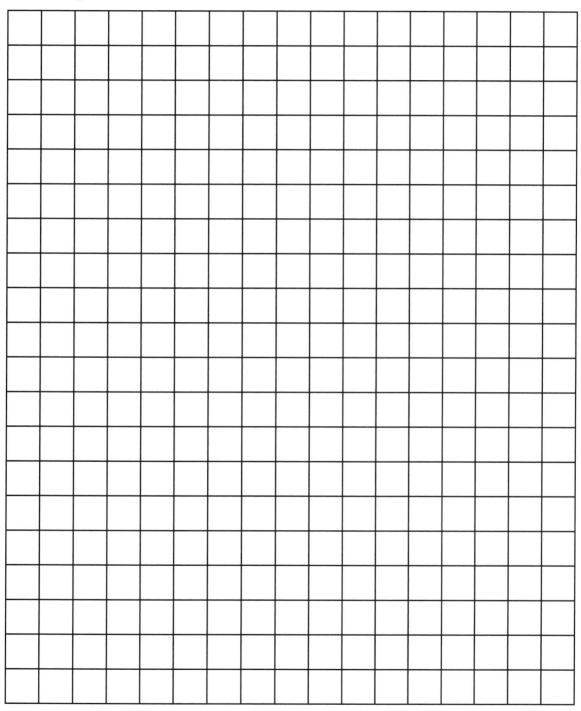

Tiling Rectangles

How many different rectangles can you make that are

$\frac{1}{4}$ blue $\frac{5}{12}$ green and $\frac{1}{3}$ red?

Draw each rectangle you find. Label the area and fraction names for each color in the rectangles.

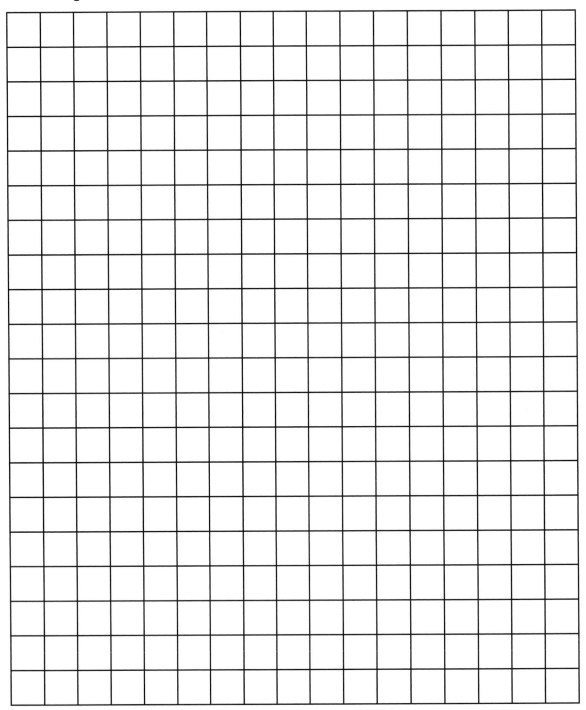

Tiling Rectangles

How many different rectangles can you make that are

$$\frac{1}{5} \text{ yellow} \quad \frac{2}{4} \text{ red and } \frac{3}{10} \text{ green?}$$

Draw each rectangle you find. Label the area and fraction names for each color in the rectangles.

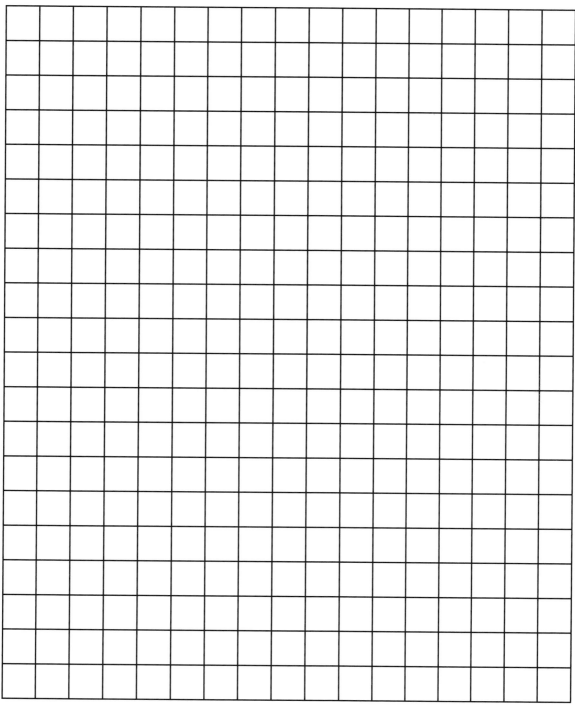

Tiling Rectangles

How many different rectangles can you make that are

$$\frac{2}{5} \text{ blue, } \frac{3}{8} \text{ green, and the rest yellow?}$$

What fraction is yellow?

Draw each rectangle you find. Label the area and fraction names for each color in the rectangles.

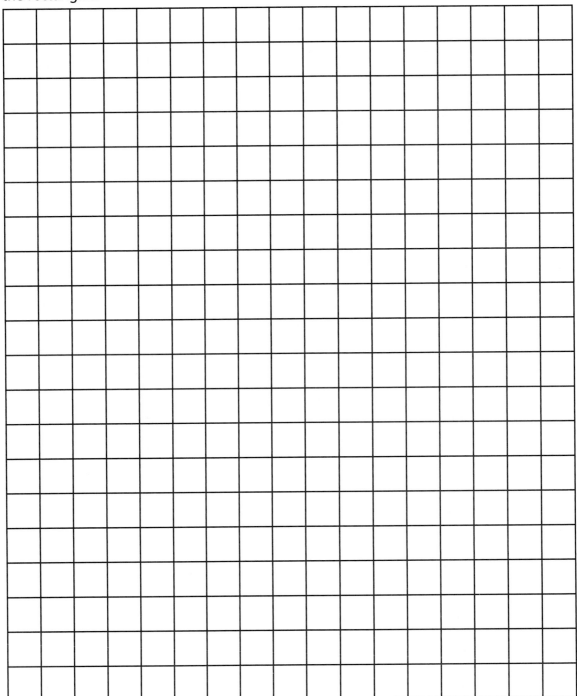

Mindset Mathematics, Grade 4, copyright © 2017 by Jo Boaler, Jen Munson, Cathy Williams.
Reproduced by permission of John Wiley & Sons, Inc.

BIG IDEA 7

Illustrating Multiplication and Division

Two researchers from England (Gray & Tall, 1994) studied students' number strategies, and they found something important: the difference between low- and high-achieving children between the ages of 7 and 13 was not that the high achievers knew more but that they had learned to be flexible with numbers. When they saw arithmetic problems, they broke numbers apart to make "friendly numbers," such as multiples of 10. Being flexible with numbers is extremely helpful when working with multiplication and division—knowing, for example, that when given a problem such as 17×19, one way to work it out is to multiply 17×20 and subtract 17. That is an example of number flexibility, which is a critical component of number sense. The big idea Illustrating Multiplication and Division helps students not only develop number sense and number flexibility but also see the relationships of multiplication and division.

In the Visualize activity, students are asked to look at some different visual representations of multiplication problems and then to make their own visual proofs of some mathematical expressions. Color coding is really important in this activity—and will help students make connections between numbers and visual representations, again encouraging the brain connections that I discussed in the notes for Big Idea 1 and in the introduction to the book. This activity is an ideal opportunity to highlight different useful strategies that students may employ, such as doubling, halving, or compensation. Students will also be asked to attend to the different features of one another's work and to revise their work. This is an opportunity to make connections between the work they do as writers—revising their work—and the work they are doing as mathematical thinkers. Often when mathematics is presented by mathematicians, it looks as though the author of the mathematical work proceeded in a linear and efficient way from a question to a solution. But this is not the case, and mathematician Imre Lakatos, in *Proofs and Refutations,* talks about the nature of mathematical work as a process of "conscious guessing" about relationships among quantities and shapes, with proof following a "zigzag" path starting from conjectures and moving to the examination of premises through the use of counterexamples or "refutations" (Lampert, 1990, p. 30).

The zigzagging nature of mathematical work, with mathematicians guessing about relationships and examining different ideas, is not well known, but could really help students value their mathematical thinking. I would suggest pointing out to students that offering and revising ideas is real mathematical work.

In our Play activity, students are asked to place rectangles on a game board, which they choose from different combinations of numbers they roll on a set of dice. This again encourages number flexibility and connections between visual and symbolic numbers. It also introduces the need for strategic thinking. As the students choose and place rectangles, they will need to think strategically to cover the board, which is something to highlight for them as they start to play their games. The game provides many opportunities for conversations about numbers, multiplication, and the commutative and associative properties.

In our Investigate activity, students are invited to spend time thinking about division as an area problem with rectangles. They are given the area and the length of one side and their goal is to find the missing side using a visual model to record their progression. We like to think of this model as a visual display of partial quotients. Students will have freedom to be creative in how they choose to build the rectangle to complete the area. When the rectangle is complete they will transfer their visual proof into number sentences to show another mathematical representation. This process supports students building connections between visual and numerical pathways in the brain. Their attention to this lesson will help students create a deeper understanding of the operation of division.

Jo Boaler

Visual Proof

Snapshot

In this activity, students will explore the connections between visual and numerical models for multiplication. Students create their own models as visual proofs. Students engage in a feedback and revision process of this work, just as mathematicians do.

Connection to CCSS
4.NBT.5
4.OA.5

Agenda

Activity	Time	Description/Prompt	Materials
Launch	15 min	Show students the problem 24 × 5 and the four visual proofs that go with it. Tell students to study the proofs and determine whether the proofs are valid.	• Handout of 24 × 5 and four solutions to show on projector, or chart reproducing the handout solutions in color • Optional: handout of 24 × 5 and the four solutions, one per student or pair
Explore	20+ min	Students work in groups to construct visual proofs for multiplication problems, drawing on the examples in the launch as models.	• One different math expression per group from the Problem Bank • Chart paper and markers for each group
Gallery Walk	10 min	Students post their proofs. In groups, students walk around and offer feedback using sticky notes, noting features of the proof that are clear, confusing, or have potential with revision.	• Posters of student proofs hung around the room • Sticky notes for each group
Revise	5–10 min	Groups take their own poster, review feedback, and make revisions to strengthen their proof.	

(Continued)

Activity	Time	Description/Prompt	Materials
Discuss	20 min	Gather all students to discuss the features of their own and others' work that made the proofs clear and understandable. Make an anchor chart with students naming the features of clear visual proofs that they identify.	Chart for recording
Explore	15+ min	Each group receives a revised visual proof from another group and investigates its validity. Students should be ready to explain the proof to the class.	Student poster proofs
Discuss	15+ min	Each group presents the proof they investigated and explain either how it works or what it would need to work.	Student poster proofs

To the Teacher

This lesson will extend across two (or more) days, giving students more time to grapple with and refine work with visual proofs. There are a few things about facilitating this lesson to consider. First, we use color strategically in the proof models shown in the launch to draw connections between illustrations and numbers. If you don't have access to color copying or printing, consider how you will share these examples with color. You might re-create them on a chart using colored markers or project them using a document camera or smartboard.

Second, revision is an important part of this lesson, and an underused practice in mathematics classrooms. Mathematicians engage in revision as a central part of developing their thinking, and students often engage in revision in writing. Make connections for students between the work they do as writers and the work they can do as mathematicians. To promote this practice, be sure to recognize and highlight when students revise their thinking or their work.

Lastly, a note on selecting numbers for this activity. We have provided a Problem Bank to get you started, but you may want to generate your own. Different numbers provide different challenges and can enable more variety in the visual models. Generally, composite numbers create more possibilities than primes.

Multiplying when both numbers are multidigit is more complex and offers more possible pathways than multiplying by a single-digit number. A number just below a landmark number (for instance 39 is close to 40 and 24 is close to 25) offers the opportunity for compensation as an efficient strategy. This kind of strategy, where students find a larger product and subtract the extra portion, is illustrated in Figure 7.1. When multiplying by a single digit, 6s, 7s, and 8s are often far more challenging than other numbers, with 7s typically being the most challenging. All of these factors can be taken into consideration when you create your own problems or select from those in the Problem Bank.

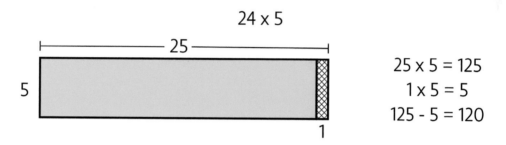

Figure 7.1

Activity

Launch

Launch this lesson by asking students to make sense of a set of visual proofs. Show the visual proofs for 24 × 5 (on either a chart or projector) one at a time and ask students if they can make sense of the problem. Have students talk with a partner and explain how the visual is showing a solution to 24 × 5. This may take some students time, so don't feel the need to rush. Ask students to share what they have found and be sure to let students come up to the class chart to point and touch to make connections. The goal is to show connections between the math expressions and the visual.

After you have made sense of all the proofs, ask the class, What makes these visual solutions clear? You may not need to use all of the proofs—enough that you feel confident that students understand how the visual proofs work. Ask students, What helped you make sense of the proofs? Be sure that students note the use of color, making connections between the pictures and numbers. If students are unfamiliar with area models for multiplication, they may need a lot of time to make sense of the pictures, and they may benefit from additional examples with smaller numbers.

Explore

Assign each group one problem from the Problem Bank. See "To the Teacher" for thoughts on complexity. Ask each group to make visual proofs on a poster to show and justify the answer. Tell them they can use rectangles and squares to make a visual proof. The poster should include the problem and the drawing that shows the visual solution of the problem. Encourage students to use color coding in the drawing and connect the color coding to the math expressions. The goal is to make the proof convincing to others.

Gallery Walk

Ask students to post their proof posters around the classroom. Tell students that they will be walking around as a group to look at the proofs others have developed. The following are guiding questions for this gallery walk:

- How did they make their proof particularly clear?
- What questions do you have about the proof?
- What suggestions do you have to the group for how to make their proof clearer or easier to understand?

Give groups some sticky notes to record their feedback. Encourage students to make their feedback specific and to place the sticky notes on the poster in the spot where the feedback makes sense. For example, if the students think a particular part is confusing, place the sticky note with their question on this spot. You may want to talk about what kinds of feedback are helpful, specific, and clear, if students do not have experience with offering feedback in this way.

Revise

Offer posters back to the groups that created them. Students should take a few minutes to review all the feedback and discuss how they could revise their poster to make it clearer or easier to understand. Encourage revision as an important part of the mathematical process. Students might simply add on to their current poster or even create a new version, if they want to make new visuals.

Discuss

Gather all students together to discuss the following questions:

- What makes a visual proof particularly clear and understandable?
- What features on the different posters did you appreciate? Why were they useful?
- What kinds of things did you revise? Why? What do you think your revisions did for your proof?

As you identify features that make a proof particularly clear, effective, or understandable, add these to a class chart that students can use as a reference for future work.

Explore

Offer each group the revised poster from another group. Their goal is to try to understand the visual proofs offered on the poster and decide whether they are valid. Groups should consider the following:

- What is going on in the proof? How did the group solve the problem?
- Does the solution work? Why or why not?
- If the solution doesn't work, what would need to happen to make it work? Is there something missing or something that needs to be revised?
- How would you explain this proof to others?

Groups should prepare to explain the proof, whether it works and why, and any suggestions for making it work if it does not.

Discuss

Each group presents to the class the solution they studied. Their presentation should address the following questions:

- What is happening in this proof?
- How and why does the solution work (if it does)?
- What would be needed to make it work (if it does not yet work)?
- Why was it convincing?

Look-Fors

- **Do students appear to connect the visual diagram to the mathematical expression?** Ask probing questions about how the two are connected if these connections are not apparent. Encourage students to use color, arrows, or other features to make these connections clear.
- **How are students breaking the numbers apart and illustrating the parts in the visual diagram?** Note the kinds of strategies that students are using to decompose, including using place value, doubling or halving, compensation, friendly numbers, or combinations of these.
- **Are students reading others' visual proofs with understanding?** Interpreting the diagrams made by others (including the models in the launch) requires a different kind of mathematical reading than students typically practice. You might find it supportive to ask students what they think the creators of the proof did first, then next, and so on.
- **Are students able to see the answer to the number expression in the visual diagram?** Orient students to how to make sense of the diagram not just as a process but as a solution. The solution is the sum of the areas of any smaller rectangles, except in a compensation strategy, where subtraction is needed. This may be difficult to understand and will require some discussion about how this works and why.

Reflect

How do the visual models of multiplication help you understand how to multiply?

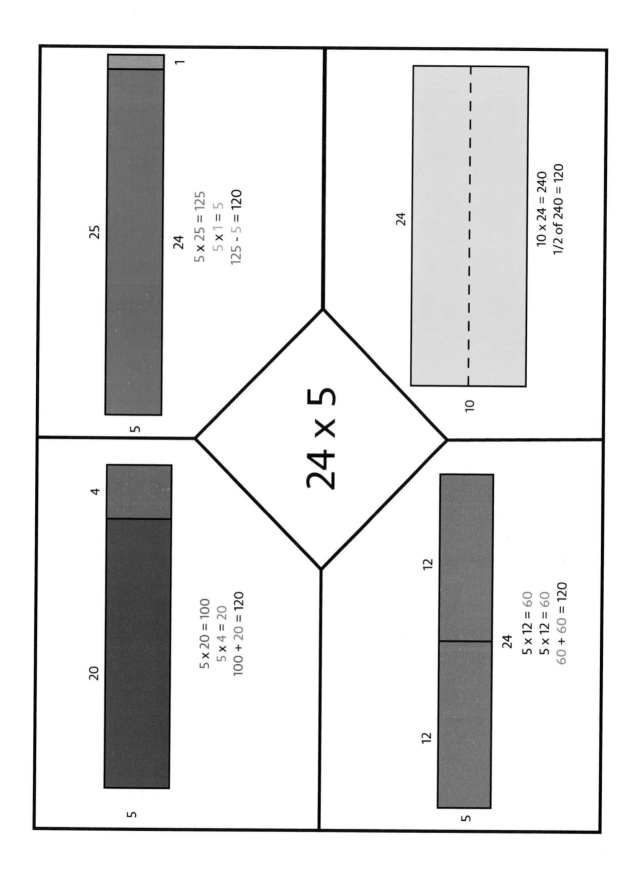

Problem Bank

36 x 8	78 x 6
295 x 4	124 x 9
1,132 x 5	2,519 x 4
45 x 19	16 x 32
51 x 22	39 x 25

Mindset Mathematics, Grade 4, copyright © 2017 by Jo Boaler, Jen Munson, Cathy Williams.
Reproduced by permission of John Wiley & Sons, Inc.

Cover the Field

Snapshot

Students play with the idea of decomposing rectangles by trying to "cover the field"—a large array—with smaller rectangles they create by rolling dice. Students must think flexibly about what rectangles they make and how they fit them into their field.

Connection to CCSS
4.NBT.5
4.OA.1
4.OA.4

Agenda

Activity	Time	Description/Prompt	Materials
Launch	10 min	Remind students of the work we've done with decomposing rectangles. Model game play and how to record equations for each turn.	Cover the Field Recording Sheet and three dice, to model the game
Play	30 min	Students play Cover the Field in partners, in which they roll dice, decide on the dimension of rectangles, and use those rectangles to cover an array as completely as they can.	• Four dice per partnership • Cover the Field game board, one per student • Cover the Field Recording Sheet, half sheet per student • Rulers (optional)
Discuss	10+ min	Discuss the strategies students developed and how students made decisions about how to use their dice rolls to create rectangle dimensions.	

To the Teacher

The focus of this game is to build on the decomposing that students have begun with rectangles. Now students must think flexibly about how to create rectangles that best fit the available space on their grid. We have written the game rules with the idea that students will sum two of the dice to create one dimension of the rectangle and sum the other two dice for the other dimension. For instance, if a player rolls 5, 3, 2, and 1, the following rectangles are possible:

$$(5 + 3) \times (2 + 1) = 8 \times 3 = 24$$
$$(5 + 2) \times (3 + 1) = 7 \times 4 = 28$$
$$(3 + 2) \times (5 + 1) = 5 \times 6 = 30$$

Students will need to record their equations, and we recommend that they record them as we have here. This is a good opportunity to introduce the use of parentheses. One adaptation that will make the game both more challenging and flexible is to offer the option for students to find either the sum or the difference between two dice to make one dimension of the rectangle. This would mean, for example, that if a player rolled 5, 3, 2, and 1, they could make the rectangles listed earlier, or they could make the following additional rectangles:

$$(5 - 3) \times (2 + 1) = 2 \times 3 = 6$$
$$(5 - 2) \times (3 + 1) = 3 \times 4 = 12$$
$$(3 - 2) \times (5 + 1) = 1 \times 6 = 6$$
$$(5 - 3) \times (2 - 1) = 2 \times 1 = 2$$
$$(5 - 2) \times (3 - 1) = 3 \times 2 = 6$$
$$(3 - 2) \times (5 - 1) = 1 \times 4 = 4$$

Note that these smaller rectangles come in handy as the game board becomes filled and smaller spaces become hard to fill. You might choose to play the original version of this game on the first day and then offer this adaptation on a second day. You will need to use the Challenge Recording Sheet and show students how to put the operation symbol of their choice ($+$ or $-$) in the empty parentheses. If you do use this variation, you will want to discuss with students how playing with subtraction changed how they thought about their decisions and how the games ended.

Activity

Launch

Launch this game by reminding students of the work they have been doing to think flexibly about finding the area of rectangles as ways to multiply. In today's game, Cover the Field, we'll be playing with covering a large array with smaller rectangles. Model the game play with students on a projector or board. Be sure to highlight for students the decisions they will need to make in trying to cover their fields and how to record an equation for each rectangle they make. You will want to give specific attention to how to use the parentheses in the equation.

Play

To play Cover the Field, each student will need a partner, a Cover the Field game board, and a recording sheet. The partnership will need four (six-sided) dice. The goal of the game is to cover your field as completely as you can.

Game Directions

- Players take turns. On your turn, roll the four dice.
- Use the values shown on the four dice to come up with the length and width of the rectangle you want to make. You must choose how to make two pairs of dice add together to become each side of the rectangle.
  - For instance, if you roll 6, 4, 3, and 1, you might choose to sum $4 + 3$ to get a side of 7 and $6 + 1$ to get a side of 7. Your rectangle would then be 7×7. Or you could sum $3 + 6$ to get a side of 9 and $4 + 1$ to get a side of 5. Your rectangle would then be 9×5.
  - You need to think about what rectangles you can make and which would be most useful in covering your field.
- Once you decide on the rectangle you want to make with your dice, draw your rectangle on your field in any place you want. You may not overlap with any existing rectangle. You may not break up your rectangle into smaller pieces.

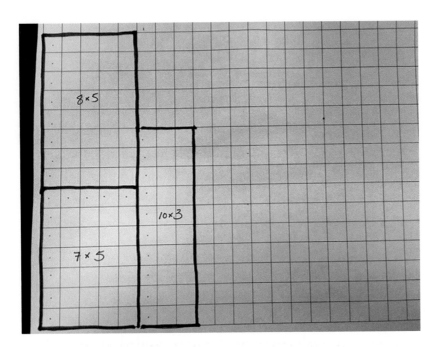

- Label and record. Label the dimensions of your rectangle on your field. Record the equation you created to find the dimension and area of your rectangle on the recording sheet.
- Game play ends when one player rolls the four dice and cannot make any rectangle that will fit on their field.
- To determine the winner, find the total area of the field you have covered. How many squares did you cover? The player who covers the greatest area wins.

Discuss

Gather students together to discuss the following questions:

- How did you decide how to use your dice to make a rectangle? What were you thinking about?
- How did your decisions change from the beginning of the game to the end of the game?
- If you wanted to make the biggest rectangle you could, how would you use your dice?
- If you wanted to make the smallest rectangle you could, how would you use your dice?
- What made this game challenging for you? How did you handle that challenge?

- How was this like our work with visualizing multiplication? How was it different?

Look-Fors

- **Are students considering the different ways they might use the dice?** Some students might automatically pair and add the dice without considering all their options. Encourage students to look at the different rectangles they might make in order to decide which is the best strategic choice for their field.
- **Are students placing the rectangles strategically?** Are they considering what orientation makes the most strategic sense? Some students might get stuck thinking that the longer dimension must be horizontal, but they can orient the rectangle either way. Encourage students to think flexibly about the commutative property: $4 \times 11 = 11 \times 4$.
- **Are students thinking about ways to maximize and minimize rectangular areas?** At the beginning of the game, making large rectangles makes sense. Are students trying to make the largest they can? How are they thinking about that? Near the end of the game, when spaces get small, making small rectangles may make more sense. How are students thinking about using the dice to make a small rectangle?
- **How are students finding the total area covered?** Students might sum the rectangles or sum the results from the equations. Others might find the un-covered area and subtract.

Reflect

What advice would you give to someone who was going to play this game?

Cover the Field

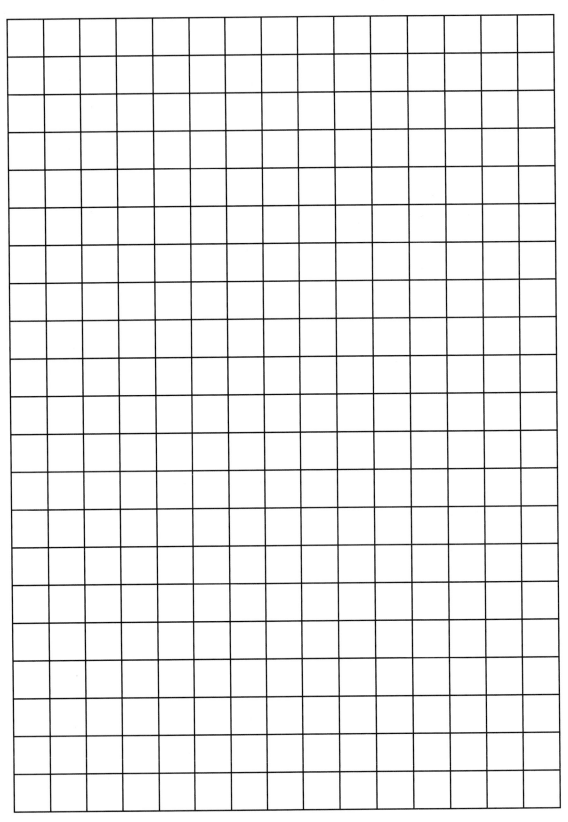

Mindset Mathematics, Grade 4, copyright © 2017 by Jo Boaler, Jen Munson, Cathy Williams.
Reproduced by permission of John Wiley & Sons, Inc.

Cover the Field Recording Sheet

1. (___ + ___) x (___ + ___) = ___ x ___ = ___

2. (___ + ___) x (___ + ___) = ___ x ___ = ___

3. (___ + ___) x (___ + ___) = ___ x ___ = ___

4. (___ + ___) x (___ + ___) = ___ x ___ = ___

5. (___ + ___) x (___ + ___) = ___ x ___ = ___

6. (___ + ___) x (___ + ___) = ___ x ___ = ___

7. (___ + ___) x (___ + ___) = ___ x ___ = ___

8. (___ + ___) x (___ + ___) = ___ x ___ = ___

9. (___ + ___) x (___ + ___) = ___ x ___ = ___

10. (___ + ___) x (___ + ___) = ___ x ___ = ___

11. (___ + ___) x (___ + ___) = ___ x ___ = ___

12. (___ + ___) x (___ + ___) = ___ x ___ = ___

13. (___ + ___) x (___ + ___) = ___ x ___ = ___

14. (___ + ___) x (___ + ___) = ___ x ___ = ___

15. (___ + ___) x (___ + ___) = ___ x ___ = ___

16. (___ + ___) x (___ + ___) = ___ x ___ = ___

17. (___ + ___) x (___ + ___) = ___ x ___ = ___

18. (___ + ___) x (___ + ___) = ___ x ___ = ___

19. (___ + ___) x (___ + ___) = ___ x ___ = ___

20. (___ + ___) x (___ + ___) = ___ x ___ = ___

---

1. (___ + ___) x (___ + ___) = ___ x ___ = ___

2. (___ + ___) x (___ + ___) = ___ x ___ = ___

3. (___ + ___) x (___ + ___) = ___ x ___ = ___

4. (___ + ___) x (___ + ___) = ___ x ___ = ___

5. (___ + ___) x (___ + ___) = ___ x ___ = ___

6. (___ + ___) x (___ + ___) = ___ x ___ = ___

7. (___ + ___) x (___ + ___) = ___ x ___ = ___

8. (___ + ___) x (___ + ___) = ___ x ___ = ___

9. (___ + ___) x (___ + ___) = ___ x ___ = ___

10. (___ + ___) x (___ + ___) = ___ x ___ = ___

11. (___ + ___) x (___ + ___) = ___ x ___ = ___

12. (___ + ___) x (___ + ___) = ___ x ___ = ___

13. (___ + ___) x (___ + ___) = ___ x ___ = ___

14. (___ + ___) x (___ + ___) = ___ x ___ = ___

15. (___ + ___) x (___ + ___) = ___ x ___ = ___

16. (___ + ___) x (___ + ___) = ___ x ___ = ___

17. (___ + ___) x (___ + ___) = ___ x ___ = ___

18. (___ + ___) x (___ + ___) = ___ x ___ = ___

19. (___ + ___) x (___ + ___) = ___ x ___ = ___

20. (___ + ___) x (___ + ___) = ___ x ___ = ___

Cover the Field Challenge Recording Sheet

1. (_____) x (_____) = _____ x _____ = _____

2. (_____) x (_____) = _____ x _____ = _____

3. (_____) x (_____) = _____ x _____ = _____

4. (_____) x (_____) = _____ x _____ = _____

5. (_____) x (_____) = _____ x _____ = _____

6. (_____) x (_____) = _____ x _____ = _____

7. (_____) x (_____) = _____ x _____ = _____

8. (_____) x (_____) = _____ x _____ = _____

9. (_____) x (_____) = _____ x _____ = _____

10. (_____) x (_____) = _____ x _____ = _____

11. (_____) x (_____) = _____ x _____ = _____

12. (_____) x (_____) = _____ x _____ = _____

13. (_____) x (_____) = _____ x _____ = _____

14. (_____) x (_____) = _____ x _____ = _____

15. (_____) x (_____) = _____ x _____ = _____

16. (_____) x (_____) = _____ x _____ = _____

17. (_____) x (_____) = _____ x _____ = _____

18. (_____) x (_____) = _____ x _____ = _____

19. (_____) x (_____) = _____ x _____ = _____

20. (_____) x (_____) = _____ x _____ = _____

---

1. (_____) x (_____) = _____ x _____ = _____

2. (_____) x (_____) = _____ x _____ = _____

3. (_____) x (_____) = _____ x _____ = _____

4. (_____) x (_____) = _____ x _____ = _____

5. (_____) x (_____) = _____ x _____ = _____

6. (_____) x (_____) = _____ x _____ = _____

7. (_____) x (_____) = _____ x _____ = _____

8. (_____) x (_____) = _____ x _____ = _____

9. (_____) x (_____) = _____ x _____ = _____

10. (_____) x (_____) = _____ x _____ = _____

11. (_____) x (_____) = _____ x _____ = _____

12. (_____) x (_____) = _____ x _____ = _____

13. (_____) x (_____) = _____ x _____ = _____

14. (_____) x (_____) = _____ x _____ = _____

15. (_____) x (_____) = _____ x _____ = _____

16. (_____) x (_____) = _____ x _____ = _____

17. (_____) x (_____) = _____ x _____ = _____

18. (_____) x (_____) = _____ x _____ = _____

19. (_____) x (_____) = _____ x _____ = _____

20. (_____) x (_____) = _____ x _____ = _____

Turning It Inside Out: What's the Missing Side?

Snapshot

Students extend their thinking about using area models for multiplication to consider how they can be used for division.

Connection to CCSS
4.NBT.6
4.NBT.5
4.NBT.1
4.MD.3

Agenda

Activity	Time	Description/ Prompt	Materials
Launch	5 min	Remind students of the area models they have been using for multiplication and challenge them to adapt this model for division.	Example of an area model from the Visual Proof lesson
Explore	15–20 min	Partners work to use an area model to find the missing side length, when one side length and the area are known.	• Blank or grid paper (see appendix), charts, or whiteboards • Colors for color coding
Discuss	10–15 min	Discuss strategies the students have developed, and highlight features of work that students might want to try in the next exploration.	Student work
Explore	20+ min	Partners explore making visual models for problems in the Problem Bank. Students try to find patterns or strategies that make solving these problems efficient, simpler to understand, or easier to keep track of.	• Problem Bank, one per partnership • Blank or grid paper (see appendix) • Colors for color coding

(Continued)

Activity	Time	Description/ Prompt	Materials
Discuss	15+ min	Make a strategy gallery by posting student solutions on the wall, clustered by and labeled with the problem they represent. Discuss with students the patterns they notice across the strategies, what strategies makes solving these problems more efficient, simpler to understand, or easier to keep track of. Name this work as division and add a division number sentence to each problem cluster.	• Student work posted on the walls in groups, labeled with the problem being solved • Additional labels with division number sentences to add to the wall at the end of the discussion
Extend	15+ min	Students investigate a problem that involves a remainder. How can you represent this with the visual model?	• Blank or grid paper (see appendix) • Colors for color coding

To the Teacher

This activity easily extends across two days. You may find it useful to engage students in the first round of exploring and discussing on the first day and then continue the lesson on a second day.

This investigation challenges students to adapt the visual models for multiplication they have been working with to division situations. These adaptations will likely represent a visual partial quotients model, with students building up the area of the rectangles piece by piece. Note that we don't explicitly name this work as division until the closing discussion. Some students may recognize this immediately; others will simply approach it as a missing side problem.

As students develop strategies, value the variety and diversity among your students' thinking. Students will decompose numbers in different ways and develop new ways to label their visual representations. This is an important opportunity to build number flexibility with division and to connect multiplication and division.

Activity

Launch

Remind students of the work that we have been doing with rectangular models for multiplication by showing one example of a complete visual model from the Visualize lesson (one we made, one you made, or one students made). Tell students that in this model, we knew the lengths of the two sides, and we used the picture to try to find out the area of the rectangle. Remind students that we were asking, How many squares are inside this rectangle? Tell students that today, we are going to ask different questions: If we know the length of one side and we know the area of the rectangle, how can we find the length of the other side? How can we use the rectangle model to help us? You may want to give students a moment to turn and talk to a neighbor about how they might do this, to get their ideas flowing.

Explore

Ask students to work with a partner on the following problem:

- If we know that one of the side lengths of a rectangle is 6 and we know the area is 276 square units, what is the length of the other side?
- How can you use the visual models we've been working with to figure it out? Develop a strategy that you can explain to someone else.

Students should create a visual that they can share, either on blank paper, grid paper (see appendix), a poster, or a mini whiteboard. Color coding will help clarify the strategy they develop. Figure 7.2 shows one example of a model students might develop for this problem, building up the rectangle piece by piece until the area is 276 squares.

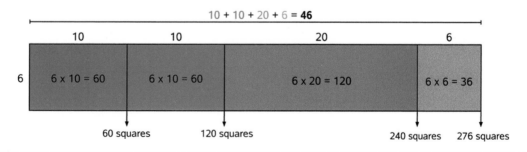

Figure 7.2

Discuss

Gather students together and ask them to share some of the different strategies and models they have developed. Be sure to highlight variety. Although some strategies may be similar, students still may have approached finding the missing side length or labeling their work differently. Discuss the following questions:

- What strategies did you develop?
- How are the models we created similar? Different?
- What strategies might you want to try next?

In this discussion, it is important to come to some shared understanding of ways that you can build out a rectangle in pieces until it has the target area and how you can then use the diagram to find the side length. Labeling is likely to be important for clarity, so be sure to highlight features of clear work that students might want to try in the next exploration.

Share the Problem Bank with students for further exploration. Invite them to try some of the useful strategies shared in this discussion.

Explore

Provide students with the Problem Bank and ask, What are some useful strategies for chunking the area to find the missing side length? Students can choose which problems from the bank they want to tackle. As students try these problems and make models, they should look for patterns that seem to make the process more efficient, simpler to understand, or easier to keep track of. Students might decide to try the same problem multiple ways, or try multiple problems. Figure 7.3 shows some examples of different ways students might come up with for chunking the area of a rectangle.

Discuss

Create a gallery of visual models by posting the different visuals partners made for each problem. Cluster models for the same problems together, with a label (for example, "Area = 276. One side = 8. What is the missing side?") to allow students to observe patterns. Label each section with the problem. Ask students to look across the different models and discuss the following questions:

- What patterns did you notice that helped you in creating your models?
- What do you notice about the different models? What stands out to you? These might be patterns, similarities, or special features.

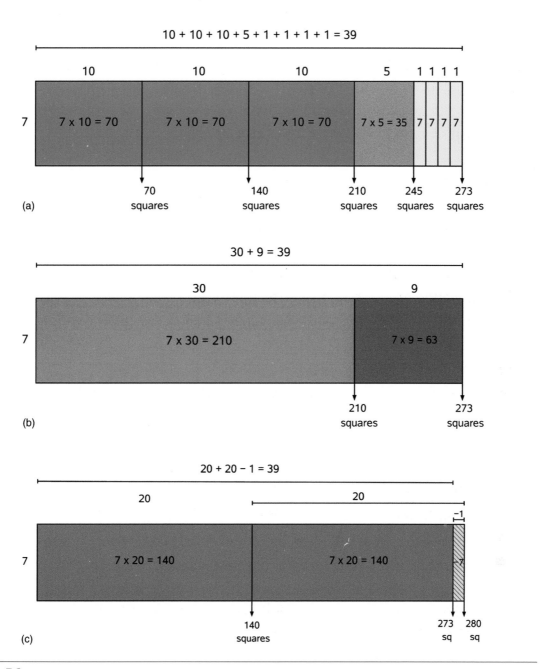

Figure 7.3

- Which models do you like the best? Why?
- Which ones help you see the missing side length? Why?
- Which models look efficient or easy to understand? Why?
- Does the order of the chunks matter? Why or why not?

If the opportunity arises, draw students' attention to the pattern that many models may start with large chunks and then taper off into smaller chunks. Ask why this is and how it might help. Also, if similar but not identical models were created, ask students how one could be transformed into the other, say by reordering or combining chunks. Close the discussion by asking students if they know what we call these kinds of problems. Students may or may not recognize that they have been dividing. Be sure to name this work as division and rename the problems they solved with division sentences. Add these labels to your gallery.

Extend

Ask students to try the final problem in the Problem Bank: Area = 283. One side = 9. This problem has a remainder and will challenge students to figure out how to deal with that remainder in their model. You can offer this to students who seem ready for a challenge or to the entire class after the closing discussion if they all seem on solid footing with using the area model to divide. Be sure to discuss what strategies they came up with and name these extra squares as the *remainder* when you discuss their models.

Look-Fors

- **Are student thinking about how to build a rectangle, inverting the process of finding the area?** Some students may find it conceptually challenging to have one side length and not the other when they try to construct a model. This is a problem of composing a rectangle, rather than decomposing. Encourage students to think about how they might build the rectangle they need bit by bit.

- **What chunks are students using to build their rectangles?** Students can, of course, build row by row, but it is far more efficient to take larger rectangles. It is often most efficient—and easiest to add—if students think in multiples of 10 or 100 first. Are students thinking about how to use place value to help them?

- **How are students labeling their work to keep track of all the pieces?** Creating a model for this work can be challenging because there are many pieces to keep track of as they go, including the growing area and the growing side length. What labeling or notation systems are students developing to help them? Encourage students to develop ways that work for them.

- **Are students taking large chunks first and then smaller pieces at the end?** This is an effective way of whittling down the area. You will be able to see this pattern in their models if the large chunks are at one end and the smaller chunks are at the opposite end. Students might notice this pattern as they look at the gallery. Be sure to get students to think about why this pattern shows up and what purpose it serves.

Reflection

How can you use a visual model to divide?

References

Gray, E., & Tall, D. (1994). Duality, ambiguity, and flexibility: A "proceptual" view of simple arithmetic. *Journal for Research in Mathematics Education, 25,* 116–140.

Lampert, M. (1990). When the problem is not the question and the solution is not the answer: Mathematical knowing and teaching. *American Educational Research Journal, 27*(1), 29–63.

Problem Bank

Area = **273** sq. units One side = **7** units What's the missing side?	Area = **747** sq. units One side = **3** units What's the missing side?
Area = **3,252** sq. units One side = **6** units What's the missing side?	Area = **2,472** sq. units One side = **8** units What's the missing side?
Area = **4,235** sq. units One side = **5** units What's the missing side?	**Extension** Area = **283** sq. units One side = **9** units What's the missing side?

Using Operations Flexibly

Successful users of mathematics have something—a comfort, a confidence—that helps them jump into any situation that needs solving and apply their mathematics knowledge. These successful students do not necessarily know more, but their approach to mathematics helps them in every learning situation. One way to encourage this approach is to present students with situations which require that they choose which method they use. When we only ever teach students by showing them methods that they practice, they never learn to make choices about methods or to enter a mathematical situation with the realization that they can make decisions about the mathematical direction.

In the Visualize activity, we invite students to make choices about operations and to use them flexibly to get results. Students are given some different photographs of crowds and asked to work out estimates for the numbers of people in the photographs. This requires that students not only make choices about operations that could help them but also estimate. In a UK government study of the mathematics that is most used in the workplace (Cockcroft, 1982), the researchers highlighted the important and often undervalued practice of estimation. They found that estimation was used more than any other part of mathematics.

Yet estimation is rarely taught in classrooms, and many students come to believe that estimation is somehow unmathematical. When students are asked to estimate, they often calculate exactly and then round the numbers! The Visualize activity provides a good opportunity to talk to students about the value and importance of estimating.

As students work to make estimates, they will make use of operations, and this provides an opportunity to highlight for them the choices they make. Encourage them to make a plan and to decide on operations, and hold discussions with them about the value of different operations.

In the Play activity, students will again be encouraged to use operations that they choose, rather than are told to use. Students will enjoy playing the game, which could be a good springboard for rich discussions with them about the methods and approaches they try. These activities are designed to give teachers opportunities to highlight flexible thinking, creative ideas, and student decision making.

In the Investigate activity, students will be given an applied problem to think about. We have deliberately suggested questions that offer students little structure, instead giving them space to make their own decisions and choices. This will give students an opportunity to be organized, make a plan, and keep careful records. We have suggested an activity—working out the number of pencils used in a school year—that has a lot of openness, with many different variables to think about. If you replace the problem with one you think of, be careful to keep the same degree of openness, and resist any urge to tell students the variables they need to think about when considering the answer. Highlight the value of keeping careful records and of making creative representations of their thinking and their results. At all times, it is useful to remind students that they are mathematical problem solvers—investigators—and that part of their role is to make decisions about topics to think about, areas to pursue, and mathematical methods to use.

Jo Boaler

How Crowded Is the Crowd?

Snapshot

In this lesson, students estimate the size of crowds from aerial photos. Thinking flexibly about operations means crafting a multistep plan employing whatever operations are useful. Estimating large quantities that cannot be counted gives students a space to make and try such plans.

Connection to CCSS
4.OA.3

Agenda

Activity	Time	Description/Prompt	Materials
Launch	5–10 min	Introduce the idea of estimating the size of a crowd of people or animals from a photo.	Photos of crowds
Explore	20–30 min	Partners work together to develop methods for estimating the size of crowds in photos. Students record their methods to justify their estimates and make their process clear.	• Photos of crowds, enough for partners to try multiple approaches • Posters and markers
Discuss	15 min	Students share and discuss the different methods they developed and whether those methods worked on different photos. Students discuss how they decided what operations to use and why those made sense in their strategy; this connects the estimation task to broader multistep problem solving.	Student posters

To the Teacher

The focus of this lesson is on thinking flexibly about operations, particularly multi-step problem-solving methods using multiple operations. By requiring estimation, the task does not give any cues to students about what operations might be necessary or even useful. Students have to reason about the task, decide on their own tools, and assemble them to achieve the goal. This is an authentic multistep problem-solving situation. Because of the nature of the task, students may see it as a lesson on estimation, which is fine. You will need to facilitate the discussion and your conversations with students along the way so that the development of the methods is foregrounded for students.

Activity

Launch

Launch this lesson by telling students that sometimes we use photos to solve problems. For instance, when there is a big event like a concert, festival, or rally, we often want to know how many attended. Photos of a crowd are used to estimate how many people were there. Scientists do the same thing with animal populations. We may want to know how many birds migrated this spring, or how many deer are in a herd. Show students some of the photos we have provided of crowds, and narrate what the photos show. How could you estimate how many people or animals are in one of these photos? Today's challenge is to develop a method for estimating and to record your methods so that others can understand how you've arrived at your estimate.

Explore

Students work in partners using a photo of their choice. Students develop a method for estimating the size of the crowd. The partners record their thinking and all their counting or calculations on a poster, making their process clear so that others can understand how they came up with their estimates. Students may want to color-code their work to make the stages in their process clear. Students can try to estimate the population in more than one picture to see if the same method works on all pictures, or if different photos require different methods. Students may want to write or draw on the photos, so you'll want to consider how you could make this possible, either by having multiple photos or by placing them in sleeves and using dry-erase markers.

Discuss

The focus of this lesson is on getting students to think flexibly and intentionally about the operations they use and how they combine them. Students will focus on their estimates and the methods they have developed, but in this discussion, you'll want to highlight how students used different operations or ordered then differently to arrive at their estimates. Ask students these questions:

- How did you arrive at your estimates? What methods did you develop?
- How did you decide to use the operations you did? Why did they make sense in your plan?

- Did anyone try something that didn't work? What did you try? How did you know it wasn't working? What did you try next?
- How did you keep track of your work? How did you organize your thinking on paper?

At the end of the discussion, draw students' attention to some of the different methods or organizational strategies that were shared. Point out that each of these methods was based on making sense of the problem, making a plan, and choosing operations and tools that would help with the plan. The task of estimating a crowd is like a lot of problems in mathematics where the problem doesn't tell you how to solve it.

This task didn't tell you to add or count or multiply or measure. You had to choose what tools to use based on how you made sense of the problem. This is one of the most important things mathematicians do.

Look-Fors

- **Are students attempting to count?** Students are often deeply uncomfortable with estimating because they have received messages about the importance of a "right" answer. In this activity, there are no right answers, only justifiable reasoning. Some students may try to circumvent the risk of being "wrong" by counting, and thus miss the point of what an estimate is and what this lesson is trying to achieve. If you encounter this hesitancy to risk being wrong, encourage students by noting that no one knows the actual answer and that it isn't important. What is important is thinking about how to estimate.
- **How are students deciding what operations or strategies (like counting or measuring) to use?** Students' decisions should be grounded in making sense of the idea of estimating. Highlight the reasoning students are using behind the decisions they are making. For instance, you might restate by saying something like, "So, you multiplied your count for this small area because you are thinking there are many spaces like it in the photo."
- **How are students using the photo to support the estimate?** Crowds often have areas that are more and less dense, and estimates will need to take this into account. Also, some photos may obscure some of the people or animals behind other objects. Is there a way for students to address this in their strategy?

Reflect

How did you decide what operations to use to come up with your estimates?

How many people are in the crowd? How many people are under the tents?

How many people are in the plaza? Are there more people or birds in this plaza?

Mindset Mathematics, Grade 4, copyright © 2017 by Jo Boaler, Jen Munson, Cathy Williams.
Reproduced by permission of John Wiley & Sons, Inc. Image by Shutterstock.com/travelview.

How many starlings are in this migration group?

How many wildebeests are in this photo? Are there other animals in this photo? How many do you think there are?

Target 20

Snapshot

Students play the game Target 20, in which players roll four dice and use operations to combine the results to get as close to 20 as they can. Students are challenged to think flexibly about using operations and how choosing different operations can lead to different outcomes.

Connection to CCSS
4.OA.3
4.NBT.4
4.NBT.5
4.NBT.6

Agenda

Activity	Time	Description/Prompt	Materials
Launch	10 min	Model game play for Target 20 and ask students to record the equations they develop in each round.	• Four dice • Target 20 Recording Sheet to display
Play	30 min	Students play Target 20 in pairs or trios, creating equations using any operations and the numbers on four dice to try to get as close to 20 as they can.	• Four dice per pair or trio • Target 20 Recording Sheet, one half sheet per player per game • Mini whiteboards and markers, one per student (optional)
Discuss	15 min	Discuss the strategies students developed and the patterns they noticed as they played that helped them get close to 20. Focus on how students recorded their equations and introduce grouping symbols to support communication.	
Extend	15+ min	Ask students to play again using a target number they choose. Or you may want to choose some other target numbers for students.	

To the Teacher

In this game, students try to get as close to 20 as they can by using different operations on the results of four dice. This game is a departure from the work students do in this big idea around estimation and problem solving, focusing instead on relationships between numbers and operations. This game can be played at any point in the sequence of this big idea to build flexibility.

The use of grouping symbols is not an explicit part of the standards until fifth grade, but this game gives rise to a natural place to discuss the need for symbols to clarify which operations come first. We encourage you to take advantage of the opportunity provided by the discussion to introduce this idea as a support in making students' equations clear. It is not necessary to explore the full extent of order of operations at this point; rather, the simple use of parentheses to make groupings clear is helpful and appropriate. Mastery of this convention is not expected. One variation of this game that may be supportive is to have students play in teams of two, collaborating to create an equation. This would mean that the game could be played by four to six players in two or three teams. This would allow students to discuss their ideas and might boost creativity.

Activity

Launch

Launch this game by rolling four dice and recording the results where students can see them readily, on a chart or board. Ask students, What numbers can we make by combining these numbers using addition, subtraction, multiplication, or division? Generate some answers and record equations to represent how students arrived at those answers. You'll want to make sure that students see examples in which both single and multiple operations are used. For instance, if you rolled 4, 2, 6, and 1, you would want an example like $4 + 2 + 6 + 1 = 13$ and one like $(4 + 2) \times 6 \times 1 = 36$.

Tell students that this is what they will be doing in today's game, Target 20, except that in this game, the goal is to get as close to 20 as you can, using all four numbers. Return to your roll and ask students to try to get as close to 20 with these numbers as they can. You may want to give students a chance to turn and talk to a partner as they generate ideas. Ask students how close they got to 20 and listen to ideas from the group. Review the rules of game play and how you want students to record their equations on the Target 20 Recording Sheet.

Play

This game can be played in pairs or trios. Each group will need four dice, and each student will need a Target 20 Recording Sheet. You may want to provide mini whiteboards and markers for students to try out their thinking and encourage revision.

Game Directions

- This game is played in 10 rounds. At the end of 10 rounds, the player with the lowest score is the winner.
- One player rolls the four dice. Dice rolling can rotate among the players.
- Once the dice are rolled, all players try to use the numbers shown on the dice to create an equation whose result is close or equal to 20. The goal is to get as close to 20 as possible.
  - Players may use any operation, in any combination.
  - There is no time limit.
  - Players must use all of the dice.
  - Players may not combine the dice as digits in a larger number. For instance, players cannot take 1 and 2 and make 12.
  - Players should record their equation on the Target 20 Recording Sheet.
- When all players have written an equation, they take turns sharing their equation and how close to 20 they got. Each player must convince the others that their way of using the dice works to get the result stated.
- Scoring: Each player's score is the distance of their result from 20. For instance, if my equation's result is 18, my score is 2, because 18 is 2 away from 20. If my equation's result is 24, my score is 4, because 24 is 4 away from 20. Players should record their score next to each round on their recording sheet.
- After 10 rounds, players find the sum of their scores. The player with the lowest score wins.

Discuss

After students have had some time to play the game, gather them together to discuss the following questions:

- What strategies did you develop for getting close to 20? What did you notice first about the numbers? What kinds of things did you try?
- How did you choose which operations to use? How did you choose what order these operations should go in?
- What was the most creative equation you came up with?
- What equations did your partner come up with that surprised you?

As students are sharing their equations, take advantage of the opportunity to introduce parentheses as ways of clarifying what operation comes first when order matters. Students will probably describe what they did by saying something like, "First, I . . ." and this can be a good opening to scribe the student's equation using parentheses to capture the student's intent. You may want to collect equations onto a Creative Ways to Get Close to 20 chart, which can serve as a model for how to record equations.

Look-Fors

- **Are students revising their thinking?** Students may want to accept their first try at creating an equation, but the goal is for students to try several different ways of using the numbers and operations flexibly to create an equation.

- **Are students making use of all operations?** Students may get in a rut of thinking about multiplication and addition, and may not think about subtraction and division. Division often gets utilized less, and it may be worth deliberately asking students, When can division help?

- **How are students recording their thinking?** Encourage students to be accurate in using the symbols they know. It can be difficult for students to translate the work they do in their head into symbolic form. Some students may need to talk it through aloud.

- **Are students stuck?** If you notice a student who is struggling to get a foothold in the game, you may want to consider offering supports like a whiteboard to try out ideas or a partner for brainstorming.

Extend

Ask students to play again using a target number they choose. Or you may want to choose some other target numbers for students.

Reflect

What advice would you offer someone who is learning to play this game? What questions do you still have?

Target 20 Recording Sheet

Round	Equation	Score
1		
2		
3		
4		
5		
6		
7		
8		
9		
10		
	Total	

Round	Equation	Score
1		
2		
3		
4		
5		
6		
7		
8		
9		
10		
	Total	

Supply Parade

Snapshot

Students extend their work with multistep problem solving and estimation to figure out how many boxes of pencils the class would use in a school year.

Connection to CCSS
4.OA.3

Agenda

Activity	Time	Description/Prompt	Materials
Launch	5 min	Orient students toward all the consumable supplies in their classroom. Pose the question, How many boxes of 12 pencils do you think we use in one school year?	A box of 12 pencils to show students (optional)
Explore	30+ min	In pairs or small groups, students work to develop a strategy for estimating the number of boxes of pencils the class will use in one year. Students gather the information they think they need to arrive at an estimate, construct a plan, and record their work to share with other.	Posters and markers for each group
Discuss	20 min	Groups present their estimates, and the class asks questions to determine how convincing the methods presented are. Students discuss the decisions they made in developing their methods. The class comes to some agreement about what the best estimate likely is.	Student posters
Extend	20+ min	Students figure out how much money the school could save by buying the class pencils from a store offering a cheaper price, rather than from a more expensive store.	Office or classroom supply catalogs (optional)

To the Teacher

This investigation focuses on crafting a strategy for estimating how many boxes of pencils the class will use in a school year. We chose this particular supply because pencils are used in every classroom, often supplied by schools, and frequently lost, and they come in packages. However, you could substitute any number of items if you think they would be of particular interest or relevance in your class. You could investigate any consumable common in your classroom and provided by the school. This could include paper, markers or other colors, soap or hand sanitizer, paper towels, tissues, staples, or milk. You will want to avoid investigating items students are responsible for purchasing, because students' financial capacity to buy supplies should not be a factor under exploration. You may want to take this opportunity to have students investigate their use of a supply of which you'd like to promote conservation, including paper, paper towels, or food.

Different items pose different challenges. Some items are used in great quantity, like paper, which can lead to working with very large numbers. Other items, like milk or hand sanitizer, cannot be counted individually. These have to be measured in some way, and this measurement will pose an additional layer of challenge. With hand sanitizer, for example, one would need to figure out how many pumps one can get from the bottle; with milk, one would need to decide what units make sense to use and how to measure consumption. This may mean that students need to physically investigate (say, by pumping lots of hand sanitizer), which requires resources. You'll want to consider these challenges when choosing an item to investigate.

The final consideration is packaging. Pencils typically come in boxes of 12, which is a relatively small number (unlike paper, which comes in reams of 500 pages). Asking about boxes of pencils opens the door for students to choose to use division or repeated subtraction, or to think multiplicatively when moving from individual pencils to packages. If you choose to substitute a different item for pencils, consider whether it makes mathematical sense for students to think about individual items or packages given the numbers that might be involved.

Activity

Launch

Launch this investigation by pointing out to students some of the supplies they use in the classroom, particularly the kinds of things that get consumed and have to be purchased again and again. Every classroom uses lots of things. You might ask students to generate examples, too. To buy all these supplies, the school has to know how much classrooms need. One thing we use a lot of is pencils. Pencils get used, lost, and broken all the time, and we always need new ones. How many pencils do you think we use in one year? You might ask students to turn and talk to a partner and come up with a quick ballpark estimate. The pencils we buy come in boxes of 12. (Show students a box of 12 pencils, if you have one.) Tell students that today you and your group will come up with a strategy for estimating how many boxes of pencils we use in this classroom in one school year. At the end of this investigation, groups will be asked to share a poster with their estimate and how they came up with it. You'll need to convince us that your estimate makes sense.

Explore

Students should work in pairs or small groups to develop a strategy to estimate how many boxes of pencils your classroom uses in one school year. Remember that each box holds 12 pencils. Start the exploration with an opportunity for groups to make a plan together before diving in. What information would you need? How could you get it? Students might want to collect some data by investigating any pencil cups or trays you have in your class, counting pencils in desks, or surveying students about how many pencils they have in their backpacks. Encourage them to collect and organize any information they think would be helpful. You might have groups share ideas for getting started or information they think they need, before sending groups off to work on the task.

Be sure to provide groups with a poster and markers. Encourage students to use color coding to help make the parts of their work clear. Posters should show their entire process and be convincing that their estimate makes sense.

Discuss

Gather students together to share their different estimates and, more important, the strategies they developed for generating these estimates. Students listening to the methods shared should be ready to ask questions to clarify or challenge the processes each group has used. Pose these questions:

- Does their strategy make sense? Can you follow all the steps?
- Could you explain what they did to someone else?
- Is their method convincing?
- Do you disagree with any part of the process? If so, why?
- Is there something they could have done to make their estimate more accurate? If so, what and why?

As students share, draw attention to the decisions students have made about what operations, information, and tools to use and the reasoning that underlies these decisions. The initial decisions students made likely had a big impact on the pathways they crafted for solving this problem. For instance, groups that thought about boxes of pencils first probably never had to divide, whereas those that thought about individual pencils had to think about how to form boxes with those pencils later.

At the close of the discussion, ask students to look again at all the posters. Thinking about all of these different methods and estimates, what do you think is the most accurate estimate? It could be one of the estimates offered or something in between. Have students share their reasoning. This is a good time to help students make sense of their estimates by making them visual. Students may try to put the numbers in order and choose the middle, or maybe combine the different class estimates and try to find a middle number. This type of thinking may not be in your fourth-grade standards; however, it is coming up in grade six. Allowing students flexibility in their thinking, and helping them organize their estimates visually are productive mathematical practices.

Extend

Pencils are not very expensive—not nearly as expensive, say, as tables or computers. But the cost of pencils can add up over time. Different stores offer slightly different prices for pencils. If one store sells boxes of pencils for $3.00 and another store sells the same boxes for $2.50, how much money would your school save by buying the pencils for your class at the cheaper store this year?

The numbers used in this extension matter. If you have not yet worked with decimals, you'll want to stick with prices that are easy to work with intuitively, like the ones given or whole dollars. However, you can adjust these prices to incorporate work with decimals. We suggest that in this case, you choose numbers that can easily add repeatedly and whose difference is straightforward to calculate, like $2.25 and $2.75.

As a further extension, you might ask, What else could be purchased for our classroom with these savings? You could give students access to an office supply catalog or other teacher resource catalog so that they can think creatively about what the savings could buy.

Look-Fors

- **What assumptions are students making as they begin? What data are they collecting?** In order to make a justifiable estimate, students will need to first come up with an idea of how many pencils are used in a shorter time frame, perhaps a week. Alternatively, they might simply figure out how many pencils are being used now and make some assumption about how quickly they need to be replaced. Each of these is a critical decision that will have a big impact on the estimates generated. It is worth probing the reasoning behind these initial estimates and assumptions to make sure students feel that these make sense and are convincing. If these aren't convincing, the estimates built on them won't be either.

- **How are students recording their process and keeping track of their intermediate calculations?** Students need an organizational system for solving a problem with so many potential parts. As you talk to students in the midst of their work, encourage them to think about how to track their work and how the poster could be a useful tool.

- **Are students thinking about the school year or the calendar year?** Student may need access to a school calendar to help them think about the difference and find out how long the school year actually is in your district.

- **Are students attending to and challenging one another's work in the discussion?** Students should be actively making sense of the different ways that other classmates arrived at their estimates and asking questions. Students should point out parts of the strategy that are not convincing and suggest things the groups could do to strengthen their estimates.

Reflect

How did you decide what operations to use to solve this problem?

Reference

Cockcroft, W. H. (1982). *Mathematics counts: Report of inquiry into the teaching of mathematics in schools.* London: Her Majesty's Stationery Office.

What Is a Decimal?

Working with numbers smaller than 1 is more difficult for students than working with numbers greater than 1. There are a few reasons for this, one of them being that numbers greater than 1 are a natural and recurring part of students' daily lives, whereas they use numbers less than 1 infrequently. In the Strategies and Errors in Secondary Mathematics Project, when students were asked to divide the number 16 by 20, a shocking 51% of 12-year-olds, 47% of 13-year-olds, 43% of 14-year-olds and 23% of 15-year-olds chose the answer "There is no number" (Kerslake, 1986, p. 4). This points to the need for students to use decimals more regularly than they do now, and to use them as a natural part of other work (rather than only in units on decimals).

A key concept for students in the learning of decimals is that relationships to the left of the decimal point hold to the right of the decimal point. Just as moving from 10 to 100 to 1,000 to the left of the decimal point means that the number is getting 10 times bigger each time, moving from one tenth to one hundredth to one thousandth to the right of the decimal point means that the number is getting 10 times smaller each time. What is difficult for many students is the fact that on the left of the decimal point, 2 is less than 16, but on the right, 0.2 is greater than 0.16. It is helpful as a teacher to know in advance that students have difficulty with this idea and therefore to give students plenty of opportunity to work with it. This concept is central to both the Play and Investigate activities in this big idea.

We launch the set of three activities in Big Idea 9 with a need for decimals. We know it is important for students to see numbers as a natural part of their world—and of course to think visually about them. Asking students to think visually about a situation that can be real for them offers them a helpful experience. You may want to change the context or bring in real examples of the unit in the activity—friendship bracelets—for them to see and feel. How do you divide a number that is less than 1? We recommend using base 10 blocks and having students draw visual proofs. As students work with physical objects, draw, and use numbers, they will be using different brain pathways and connecting between them, which is a process that increases understanding and achievement.

In our Play activity, called Decimals on a Line, students play a fun game in pairs, with the goal of plotting four decimals in a row on a number line. Students take it in turns choosing two numbers to make decimals and placing them on a number line, and they try to stop each other getting four in a row. In our trials of this activity, students really enjoyed the game and had important discussions that helped their understanding of decimals. This activity also integrates fractions with decimals as the activity starts with a fraction "number talk," and the students write their numbers as both fractions and decimals, which will help deepen their understanding of both.

In our Investigate activity, students are given the task of finding every number from 1 to 20 using only the numbers 1.25, 1.5, 2, and 4. We deliberately chose 1.25 and 1.5 so that students would get the opportunity to see that 1.25 is smaller than 1.5, correcting a common misconception. This is a creative activity because students can combine numbers in any way, using any operation. We have found that students are excited to learn about the factorial operation, particularly when it unlocks some numbers they have been searching for. It is known to be more effective to teach students content after they encounter a need for that content, rather than before they work on an activity. If students have an opportunity to try to work something out, and to struggle, their brains will experience growth and then, when they learn new content that will help them move forward, their minds will be receptive to that content, as they can see a need for it. This investigation will be exciting for students as they have freedom to create their own numbers in any way they choose, while at the same time working with decimals.

Jo Boaler

Finding the Better Deal

Snapshot

Students begin their exploration of decimals by constructing visual proofs to determine which store has the better deal on friendship bracelets. Students use their understanding of money to support their thinking about decimal numbers.

> Connection to CCSS
> 4.NF.6
> 4.NF.7
> 4.OA.3

Agenda

Activity	Time	Description/Prompt	Materials
Launch	10 min	Students generate visual ways to represent the meaning of $1.50. Students draw on these examples to think about how they might create a visual proof for today's puzzle about finding the better deal on friendship bracelets.	• Chart and markers • Task to display
Explore	30 min	Students work in small groups to determine which is the better deal on friendship bracelets if you need to buy 20 of them: 4 for $5.00 or 10 for $13.00. Each group constructs a visual proof of their solution using drawings, base 10 blocks, or money	• Finding the Better Deal sheets, one per student or partnership, or charts and markers for each partnership • Base 10 blocks (flats, longs, and cubes) • Pretend money (dollars and coins) • Optional: hundreds grids or grid paper (see appendix)

(Continued)

Activity	Time	Description/Prompt	Materials
Discuss	15–20 min	Groups present their solutions and visual proofs. The class critiques each group's reasoning and the quality of their visual proof. The class determines what kinds of representations of decimals offer the greatest clarity and precision.	Student work

To the Teacher

Base 10 blocks are useful tools for modeling decimals, particularly when we redefine which block represents one whole. When working with decimals through the hundredths place, the flat (100) can become the whole, so that the long (10) will then represent $\frac{1}{10}$ and the cube (1) represents $\frac{1}{100}$. (See Figure 9.1.) Students may struggle with how to reimagine using these tools in this way if they have never encountered thinking flexibly about what the blocks might represent. To support their use of this manipulative, you might need to encourage students to consider what could represent a dollar and then what would represent a penny. Hundreds grids or grid paper (see appendix) can then support students in recording the work they have done with these blocks and should be an optional tool.

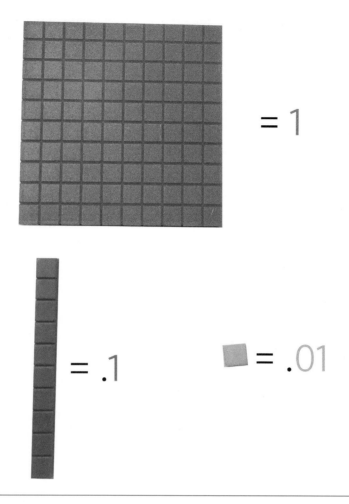

$= 1$

$= .1$

$= .01$

Figure 9.1

The discussion at the end of today's activity focuses heavily on using critique. If your students have not had experience with this process, this is a good opportunity to introduce the ways in which mathematicians discuss one another's ideas. It is important that the dialogue focuses on ideas, not people, and that students steer clear of judgmental language about how good or bad something is. Instead, you'll want to encourage students to be precise about the features of the work or reasoning they find clear or unclear, convincing or unconvincing, and, important, and why. This allows everyone to learn how to create clearer, more convincing, and more precise representations in the future, and this should be the tenor of the discourse.

Activity

Launch

Launch this activity by reminding students of situations in their community in which they often see prices—perhaps at the grocery store or the school cafeteria, signs at the gas station, or in advertisements. Usually when we see prices, they look something like "$1.50." Write this value on a chart. What pictures could we draw or what objects could we use to show what $1.50 means? Ask students to turn and talk to a partner about ways we could show what $1.50 means. Give students a few minutes to talk, and then collect their ideas. Represent their ideas on your chart. Students will likely have ideas that include using bills and coins, and drawing a whole shape and a half shape. You might specifically ask students how they could use base 10 blocks or other manipulatives to show what $1.50 means. Collect as many visual representations on your class chart as students can generate.

Tell students that today we are going to be working on a puzzle involving money, and we want to create a visual proof of our answers. This means using objects or pictures as we did in this chart to show what we've found, so that others can understand. Share with students the puzzle either by projecting the Finding the Better Deal sheet or by writing the task on a chart. Ask students to create a visual proof that shows why one store has a better price than the other. Be sure to point out to students the resources they have available, including base 10 blocks and pretend money. It is important to connect visual representations to number sentences. This is especially helpful when you use color coding.

Explore

Students work in small groups to create a visual proof of their solution for the following problem:

You are interested in which store is giving a better deal on friendship bracelets. One store is selling friendship bracelets with a sign that reads, "4 for $5.00." The store next door has a sign above their friendship bracelets that says, "10 for $13.00." Which store is offering the better price for a friendship bracelet if you need to buy 20?

Students can put their proofs on the Finding the Better Deal sheet or on chart paper. If students use manipulatives, encourage them to draw what they did so that they have a record of their thinking.

Discuss

Gather students together to discuss their visual proofs of the better deal. Invite students to share different answers and, particularly, different ways of representing their evidence visually. As groups share, ask those listening to be asking themselves these questions:

- Is the group's reasoning convincing?
- Is the visual proof convincing? Why or why not?

After each group has shared, ask the rest of the class to critique the group's reasoning and visual proof. Be sure to probe students not to evaluate how good it is but rather to focus on the specific qualities or connections that are convincing or that leave the listener with questions. During these short discussions, precision is important, and this is a valuable opportunity to highlight students' use of language, the posing of questions, and the features of clear and convincing work.

As students are sharing, draw specific attention to how they address the breaking of whole dollars into cents. This is an opportunity to offer students some decimal language—in particular, that each cent is a hundredth of a dollar. Students will also intuitively compare hundredths to hundredths, an important consideration in making comparisons in the future. That is, students are unlikely to think of the unit rate for 10 friendship bracelets for $13.00 as $1.3; instead they will naturally label this as $1.30, which makes comparing it to $1.25 far easier. When students make this leap from tenths to hundredths, ask them why this makes sense, and focus student attention on the idea that they are comparing like units (cents to cents, rather than dimes to pennies).

Finally, close the discussion by asking students which visual models were most useful for working with and comparing decimals. Be sure to highlight why some models (base 10 blocks or money) offer greater precision than others.

Look-Fors

- **Are students thinking about the price of one friendship bracelet?** The goal of this activity is to leverage students' understanding of money to think about decimal numbers. There are other valid reasoning strategies, including scaling up. However, in this case, you'll want to encourage students to seek a unit rate. You might ask students to think about what one bracelet costs at each store and how they could prove that.

- **How are students trying to find the unit price?** Make note of the different strategies students are using, including modeling with coins, base 10 blocks, or other visual strategies. Some students might first think in terms of numbers and only then try to find a representation. How are these students thinking about making equal shares? Are students estimating or thinking precisely? The values in this problem are so close that precision will be needed to prove which is the better deal. Be sure to probe student reasoning and encourage precision so that they can convince others of their thinking. Their visual models should have just as much precision as their thinking. Base 10 blocks and grid paper (see appendix) will support students in being precise.

Reflect

What model or models do you think are most useful for representing decimals? Why?

Finding the Better Deal

You want to buy 20 friendship bracelets for your friends.

One store is selling them with a sign that says:	The store next door has a sign above their friendship bracelets that says:
## 4 friendship bracelets for $5.00	## 10 friendship bracelets for $13.00

Which store is offering the better price for 20 friendship bracelets? Create a visual proof to show why one store has a better price than the other. State your reasons to justify your choice.

Mindset Mathematics, Grade 4, copyright © 2017 by Jo Boaler, Jen Munson, Cathy Williams. Reproduced by permission of John Wiley & Sons, Inc.

Decimals on a Line

Snapshot

Decimals on a Line provides students a chance to make connections between whole numbers, the operation of division, and how decimal numbers represent numbers between whole numbers.

Connection to CCSS
4.NF.3
4.NF.6
4.NF.7

Agenda

Activity	Time	Description/Prompt	Materials
Launch	10 min	Draw a number line for students. Mark 0 through 5 and ask students where the following numbers should be placed: $\frac{1}{2}$, $\frac{3}{2}$, $\frac{4}{2}$. Do this as a number talk and record all student responses.	Number line drawn on the board
Play	30 min	Students play Decimals on a Line in pairs. Each player takes a turn choosing two numbers from a given set and marking their quotient on the number line. Each player uses a unique color to record their quotients. The winner is the first to place four numbers in a row in their color on the number line. Each player should use a calculator to determine the quotient.	• Calculator • Decimals on a Line game board • Two different colored pens
Discuss	15 min	As a group, discuss strategies that students developed for selecting numbers to help them win the game.	

To the Teacher

Decimals on a Line is a game in which students divide two numbers to achieve a quotient that they will place on a number line. The goal is for students to understand that there are decimal numbers between whole numbers. Students should play using a calculator so that the focus is on the location of decimal numbers on the number line. Many of the numbers we have chosen for the game result in whole-number answers and decimal numbers to the tenth and hundredths places. A few of the calculations will result in quotients that have thousandths and ten-thousandths place values.

Activity

Launch

Make a number line for the class showing the whole numbers 0, 1, 2, 3, 4, and 5. In the number talk style, ask students where they would place the number $\frac{1}{2}$. Take student ideas and discuss as a whole class what position makes sense for $\frac{1}{2}$ on the number line. If students have conflicting ideas or present ideas without precision, such as by saying "between the 0 and 1," probe their thinking and ask other students what they think. Support the class in coming to agreement. Then ask them where they would place $\frac{3}{2}$. Give students time to turn and talk with a partner about where they would place $\frac{3}{2}$ and why. Record all the locations they share and discuss which one makes the most sense. In these discussions, highlight any use of equivalence to reason about where the fraction is placed. For instance, if students reason that $\frac{3}{2}$ is the same as $1\frac{1}{2}$, they are using an equivalent form of the number that is more useful when trying to place it on the number line.

Tell students that in today's game, they are going to use equivalence with decimals to think about where to place fractions on the number line. You might ask students if they know the decimal equivalents of $\frac{1}{2}$ and $\frac{3}{2}$ and add those labels to your number line to draw students' attention to equivalence. Share the directions for the game with students, modeling how to use the game board and record their work on each turn.

Play

Students play in pairs with one Decimals on a Line game board. Players decide who will go first.

Game Directions

- Player A picks two numbers from the group 1, 2, 4, 5, 8, 10, 16, 20, 24, and 25. Players may not pick the same number twice for their turn. For example, they cannot choose 10 and 10.
- Player A makes a fraction out of the two numbers and records it in the table on the game board.
- Player A makes the fraction into a decimal number, records the decimal number in the table, and records the number on the game board in their chosen color for recording.

- Player B takes a turn by choosing two numbers, making a fraction, recording the fraction in the table, and calculating the decimal equivalent. Player B then records the decimal number in the table, and places it on the number line.
- The goal is for a player to get four consecutive numbers on the number line in their color.
- If a player makes a decimal number that has already been recorded or is not possible to place on the number line because the line only goes to 5, the player loses their turn. The fraction they made and the calculated decimal should be recorded in the table so that players have a record of all fractions they created.

Students can play multiple rounds of this game, and will need a new game board for each round.

Discuss

Gather students together to discuss the following questions:

- What strategies helped you pick your numbers to make a fraction?
- Did you need the calculator all the time? When did it help you? When did you decide you didn't need it?
- What strategies did you use to put the decimal numbers on the number line?

Help students discuss the different decisions they were making and, especially, how they were thinking about the different forms of numbers. They may have been challenged to put the decimal number on the number line and found using the fraction representation easier. The goal is for students to realize that both representations are equivalent.

Look-Fors

- **Are students able to find the decimal value using the calculator?** If students do not have much experience with calculators, they may need support in using the buttons and reading the display.
- **Do students catch their mistakes if they reverse the order of the numbers when they use the calculator?** For example, if they are finding $\frac{1}{5}$ as a decimal but get the result of 5 on the calculator, do they notice? Encourage students to reason about where they expect the fraction to fall on the number line before entering the numbers into the calculator. Is it less than or more than 1? What whole numbers do you expect it to fall between? Why? Anticipating by

reasoning about fractions and division will support students in catching errors such as reversals and in making connections between fractions, division, and decimals.

- **Do students use any of the numbers that are possible, or do they choose only numbers they are comfortable with?** Students will likely begin with familiar numbers, but as they play the game, choosing less familiar values will likely be necessary to win. Prompt students to think about where on the number line would be useful places to mark, and to ask themselves, Which numbers might get me close?

- **How do students determine where to place the numbers on the number line?** Are they comfortable breaking the number line into equal segments between whole numbers? Do they understand how to compare numbers with tenths and hundredths? Draw on students' knowledge of money and the models they used in the Visualize activity to help them reason about the relationship between the different decimal values. Be sure to ask probing questions of all students about how they know where to place the decimals on the number line. Use areas of persistent confusion or disagreement as places to highlight in the discussion.

Reflect

Which is greater 0.4 or 0.12? Give a picture or an argument to justify your answer.

Decimals on a Line

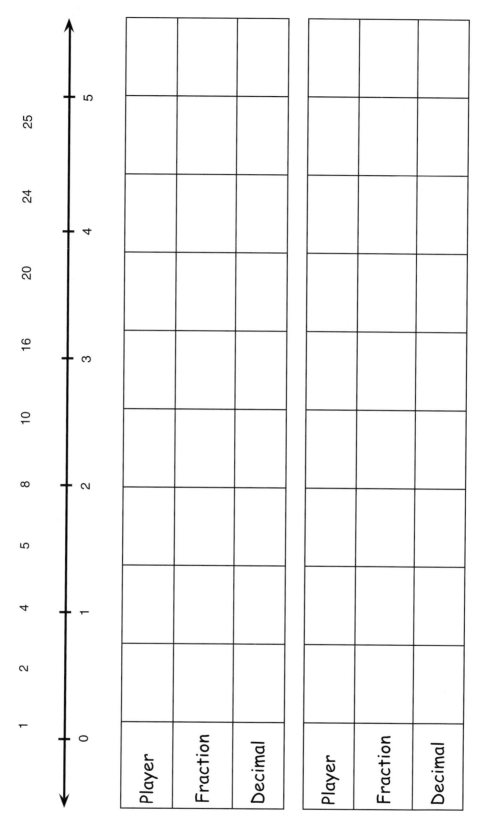

Can You Make It?

Snapshot

This investigation opens the door to thinking about how decimal numbers fit together to make whole numbers. Students investigate how to write number sentences to find the values 1 through 20, using both whole and decimal numbers.

Connection to CCSS 4.NF.6 4.NF.7	

Agenda

Activity	Time	Description/Prompt	Materials
Launch	10 min	Write the numbers 1 through 20 on the board or chart paper and ask students to consider how they might write number sentences for them. Pose the constraints of the investigation and be sure that they are clear.	Optional: charts and markers
Explore	30+ min	Students use exactly four numbers from the set of 1.25, 1.5, 2, and 4 to create number sentences for every value 1–20. Students record visual proofs for each number sentence they create.	Make available: base 10 blocks, plastic money, colors, and number lines
Discuss	15+ min	Discuss students' findings, including their number sentences and their visual proofs. Ask students to review the number sentences to see if they have any questions or if they want to be a skeptic. Reflect on what tools were useful and what values were most challenging to find.	Class chart or recording space for students' number sentences and evidence

To the Teacher

This investigation opens the door to operating with decimals. Proficiency with decimal operations is not expected in fourth grade; however, part of understanding decimal numbers is thinking about how they fit together into wholes. In this investigation, students are asked to explore how benchmark decimal numbers could be used to create whole numbers. We have chosen the numbers 1.25 and 1.5 as sites for students to begin building intuition around decimal operations because these numbers are related to the decimal equivalents of $\frac{1}{4}$ and $\frac{1}{2}$, and these are values that students will likely have experience with in the context of money. We recommend that you emphasize reasoning about and modeling these numbers with pictures, number lines, money, and base 10 blocks as entry points to making meaning about decimal operations.

Depending on the length of time your class wants to spend on exploring this puzzle, this investigation may be stretched across two or more days. It could be left on display for an extended period so that students can continue finding different ways to calculate each number.

Activity

Launch

Write the numbers 1 through 20 on the board or on chart paper. Tell students that in today's investigation, they are going to be trying to write different number sentences with each of the numbers 1 through 20 as answers. You might ask students to turn and talk about what number sentences they can write already that have these answers. Students can probably quickly think of a number sentence for any of these numbers. In this investigation, tell students that the challenge is that their number sentences must always use four numbers. And they must choose their four numbers from the following list: 1.25, 1.5, 2, and 4. Be sure to record these numbers on the board or chart. Students can use any of the numbers more than once and they may use any operation they choose. For instance, students can use sets of numbers like 4, 4, 1.5, and 2, or even 2, 2, 2, and 2. Students must show a visual proof for each of their number sentences. Share with students the manipulatives you will make available to support their thinking.

Explore

Provide students with a variety of manipulatives to represent and work with the decimals, including plastic money and base 10 blocks. Students each work on their own paper to create number sentences and visual proofs for how to use the numbers 1.25, 1.5, 2, and 4 for every answer 1 through 20. Students may use any of these numbers more than once, but they may only use four numbers in a number sentence. Students record their work on their own paper so that they have adequate room to construct visual proofs for each number sentence. Visual proofs might include number lines, money, base 10 blocks, area models, or some other student-invented model. See Figure 9.2 as an example of a visual proof.

Even though each student will work on their own paper, encourage them to talk to one another, share their models, look at each other's visual evidence, and ask questions.

Discuss

Gather students together with their visual proofs and discuss their findings. Display their visual evidence along with their number sentences for each value 1 through 20. Ask students about the strategies they used to find the numbers 1 through 20. If there are multiple ways to generate some of the numbers, ask students to compare

Examples of number sentences and their visual proofs.

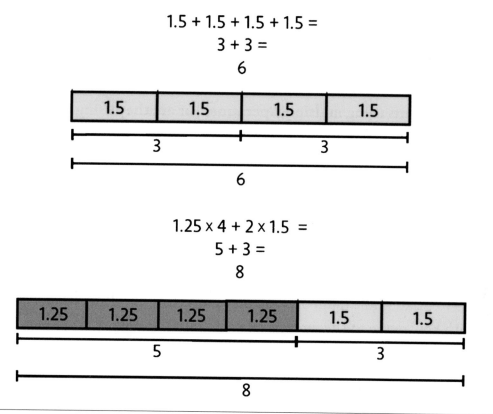

1.5 + 1.5 + 1.5 + 1.5 =
3 + 3 =
6

1.25 x 4 + 2 x 1.5 =
5 + 3 =
8

Figure 9.2

the methods that were used. Students may see mistakes. This is a good time to ask for students to be skeptics. After you have recorded students' evidence and come to agreement on the number sentences that work, discuss the following questions:

- Are there any numbers you used more than others? Why?
- What is the number that was used the least? Why?
- What answers were the most difficult to find?
- What operations were used the most? The least?
- Are there any values still missing? Do you think they are possible? Why or why not?

If there are values for which no one found a number sentence, you may want to send students back to work to find number sentences that represent these missing values.

Look-Fors

- **Are students using the decimal numbers flexibly and often?** Some students may begin their investigation by focusing on the two more familiar whole numbers; however, students will be limited in the solutions they can find if they do not include the decimal values. Encourage students to think about how they could use the decimal values to get a whole-number answer.

- **Are students using multiple operations, or are they using the same few for all their number strings?** Students may begin by thinking about addition as a way to build whole numbers from decimals. This is a useful entry point. After students have exhausted the possibilities of addition, encourage them to think about how subtraction and multiplication, in particular, could help them build whole numbers from decimals.

- **Are students connecting decimals to fractions?** Students should leverage their understanding of $\frac{1}{4}$ and $\frac{1}{2}$ to help them think about how to use 1.25 and 1.5 to make whole numbers. You may want to ask students who are struggling with how to use the decimal numbers to talk about what those numbers represent. Often getting students to name these as "one and a quarter" and "one and a half" helps them see how they could be used as building blocks.

- **What models are students choosing to explore and to prove their answers?** Models that involve money, number lines, diagrams, or base 10 blocks can be used both as evidence for proving and as tools for solving. Encourage students to think about what models help them make sense out of operating with decimals. Keep in mind that proficiency with decimal operations is not an expectation. Instead, the goal is for students to build some intuition, grounded in visuals and manipulatives, that makes sense to them. Ask students probing questions about how their models do (or could) make sense.

Reflect

What number was the most challenging number for you to find? What strategies did you use to find that number?

Reference

Kerslake, D. (1986). *Fractions: Children's strategies and errors. A report of the Strategies and Errors in Secondary Mathematics Project.* Windsor. England: NFER-Nelson.

Appendix

Centimeter Dot Paper

Appendix

Isometric Dot Paper

Grid Paper

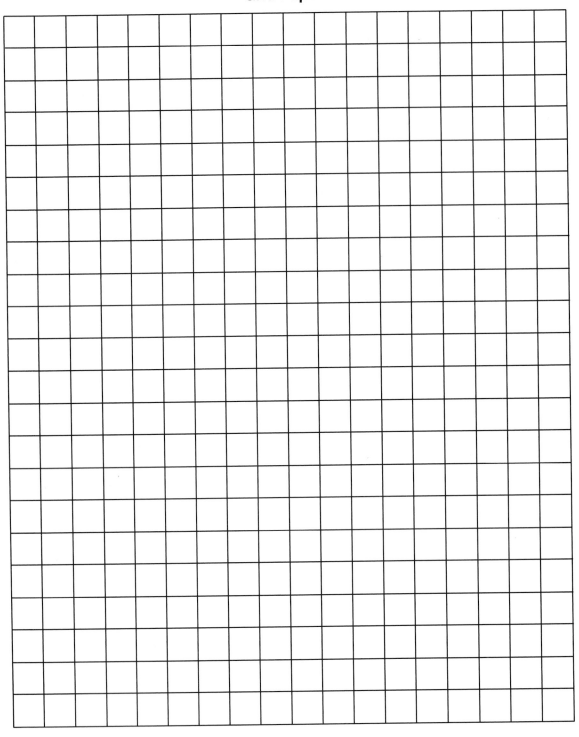

Appendix

¼" Dot Paper

¼" Grid Paper

Hundred Grids

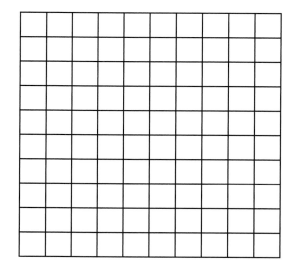
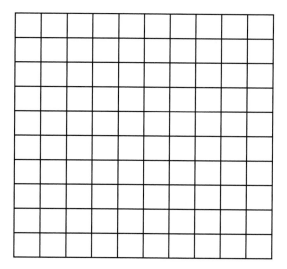
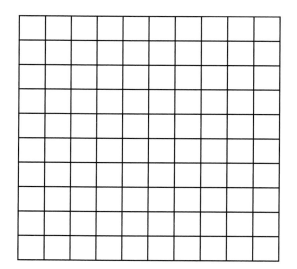
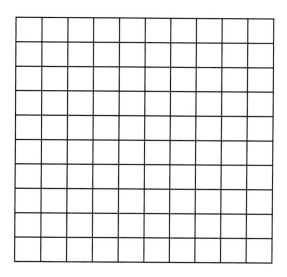

About the Authors

 **Dr. Jo Boaler** is a professor of mathematics education at Stanford University, and the cofounder of Youcubed. She is the author of the first MOOC on mathematics teaching and learning. Former roles have included being the Marie Curie Professor of Mathematics Education in England, a mathematics teacher in London comprehensive schools, and a lecturer and researcher at King's College, London. Her work has been published in the *Times,* the *Telegraph,* the *Wall Street Journal,* and many other news outlets. The BBC recently named Jo one of the eight educators "changing the face of education."

 **Jen Munson** is a doctoral candidate at Stanford University, a professional developer, and a former classroom teacher. Her doctoral research focuses on how coaching can support teachers in growing their mathematics instructional practices, particularly in the elementary grades, and how teacher-student interactions influence equitable math learning. As a professional developer, she focuses on growing teachers' and leaders' capacity to craft rich, responsive, and equitable mathematics classrooms. Before leaving the classroom to coach, she taught in elementary and middle school in Washington, D.C., Chicago, and the Seattle area.

Cathy Williams is the cofounder and director of Youcubed. She completed an applied mathematics major at University of California, San Diego before becoming a high school math teacher for 18 years in San Diego County. After teaching, she became a county office coordinator and then district mathematics director. As part of her leadership work, Cathy has designed professional development and curriculum. Her district work in the Vista Unified School District won a California Golden Bell for instruction in 2013 for the K–12 Innovation Cohort in mathematics. In Vista, Cathy worked with Jo changing the way mathematics was taught across the district.

Acknowledgments

We would like to thank Jill Marsal our book agent and Kate Bradford, our editor, two amazing women who have supported our work with grace and patience. We are also very grateful to teachers who trailed tasks for us—Haley Harrier, from Barron Park elementary, and Megan Jensen, and Pegi Hover from Valley Life Charter School. Thanks also to Shelah Feldstein and Staci Hatcher for helping to coordinate trials. Thanks to Robin Anderson who drew the network diagram that appears on our cover, and Melissa Kemmerle who assisted early in the project. And finally we would like to thank our children and dogs!—for putting up with our absences from family life as we worked to bring our vision of mathematical mindset tasks to life.

Index

exploration of, 207; launch of, 207

How Flexible Is a Number activity, 41–48; agenda for, 41; discussion for, 41, 43–44; exploration with, 41, 43; extension of, 41, 44; launch of, 41, 43

Humphreys, Cathy, 8

Hundreds Grids, 249

I

Ideas, 214, 236; building and designing with shapes and angles as, 49–70; collection of, 169, 230; color-coding for, 6; conjecture as, 89; connections between, 9; decimals as, 225–244; discussion of, 58–59, 229; of factors, 33; making and naming patterns as, 71–95; modeling with units fractions as, 115–141; operations flexibly as, 203–224; patterns inside numbers as, 23–48; play and, 13; sharing of, 34, 76, 111; support for, 93; about teachers, 14; about units, 113; units are relationships as, 97–114

Illustrations, 91, 180. *See also* Drawings; Photos

Information: communication of, 106; graphs as, 99, 101; numbers as, 23; organization of, 221; recording of, 98

International Student Assessment (PISA), 4

Intuition, 244

Investigate activities, 24, 50, 98, 117, 144, 178; Collatz conjecture as, 72

investigation, 42; challenges of, 196; collection of, 117; data from, 112; as physical, 220; of polyiamonds, 64; teachers and, 111; time for, 168, 241

Isometric Dot Paper, 247

It's All in the Axes activity, 99–103; agenda for, 99; discussion for, 99, 101; exploration as, 99, 101; launch of, 99, 101

J

Journals: materials as, 240; mathematical thinking and, 5–6

K

Kelly, Ellsworth, 150, 151

L

Labels, 78, 200; accuracy of, 123; for fractions, 160, 169, 173–176; recording and, 190; for units, 121

Lakatos, Imre, 178

Language, 231

Launch: of All Hail! activity, 88, 90–91; of Can You Make It? activity, 240, 242; for Color Coding Fractions activity, 157, 159; of Cover the Field activity, 187, 189; of Decimals on a Line activity, 234, 236; of Finding Fibonacci activity, 74, 76; of Finding the Better Deal activity, 227, 230; of How Crowded is the Crowd activity, 207; of How Flexible Is a Number activity, 41, 43; of it's All in the Axes activity, 99, 101; of Measure Up activity, 104, 106; of Painting Pieces activity, 145, 147; of Pattern Carnival activity, 83, 85; of Perplexing Measures activity, 118, 120–121; of Pixeled Fractions activity, 132, 134; of Supply Parade activity, 221; of Tangram Designs, 124, 126; of Target 20 activity, 215; of 10,000 Steps activity, 110, 112; of Those Crazy Rep-Tiles activity, 56, 58; of Tile It! activity, 51, 53; of Turning It Inside Out activity, 197; of Visual Proof activity, 179, 182; of Visualizing Numbers activity, 28; of What Could It Be activity, 33, 34

Learning: of decimals for students, 225–244; fractions for students, 116, 159

Length, 199

Leonardo of Pisa, 74

Lessons: extensions for, 100; facilitation of, 180–181; focus of, 206, 207; teachers about, 84, 89, 105, 119, 180

Line plots: data on, 108; posters with, 104, 105, 106

Lines, 136, 139, 140

Lockhart, Paul, 8, 49

M

Manipulatives, 126, 230; materials as, 41; variety of, 242

Mason, John, 8

Materials: for activities, 41, 51, 56, 63, 77, 83, 99, 132; challenges of, 220; charts as, 63, 66, 74, 104, 107; dice as, 187, 189, 190, 191, 213; journals as, 240; manipulatives as, 41; paper as, 18, 19–21, 121, 133, 161; pencils as, 219; photos as, 205; for WIM, 12

Math anxiety, 2

Mathematical reading, 184

Mathematical thinking, 14, 92; journals and, 5–6; students and, 178

Mathematicians, 71; Devlin as, 72; discussion for, 229

Mathematics, 71; expressions of, 177, 182, 184; as imaginary, 97; opening of, 13; visuals and, 10–13; in workplace, 203

Mathematics: The Science of Patterns (Devlin), 72

Measure Up activity, 104–109; agenda for, 104–105; discussion for, 104, 107; extension for, 105, 107; launch of, 104, 106; play as, 104, 107

Measurement: accuracy of, 108; of consumption, 220; discussion of, 119; nonstandard units of, 104–109; by students, 118–123;

tools for, 120; units and, 97, 114; verification of, 122

Measurement (Lockhart), 49

Memorization, 4–5

Menon, Vinod, 10

Methods, 7, 203

Mindset Mathematics Series, 9

Mistakes, 35, 237, 243

Models, 238; connections between, 179–202; for decimals, 228; for division, 195; for multiplication, 195; patterns and, 199, 200; peers as, 111; reasoning and, 241; rectangles as, 197; visual proofs as, 179–186, 226, 230

Modifications, 135; of solutions, 129

Mondrian, Piet, 154, 155

Money, 227, 238; context of, 241; puzzles about, 230; representations of, 228

Moniamond, 64, 68

Multiplication: division and, 177–202; models for, 195; representations of, 177

N

Nature: Fibonacci in, 75, 77; mathematics and, 73. *See also* Animals

Neuroscience: findings from, 14; research in, 10–11

Norm building, 17–21

Number lines, 11, 116, 238; fractions on, 118–123

Number sentences, 240–244

Numbers, 159, 215, 225; for Activities, 181; as composite, 44; decomposition of, 42, 128; extensions use of, 222; flexibility and, 41–48, 196; groups of, 28; illustrations of, 180; as information, 23; as landmark, 181; making and naming patterns of, 71–95; as multidigit, 181; order of, 11; patterns inside, 23–48; relationships between, 30; representations of, 232; as sequences, 88, 91; symbols as, 25; visuals and, 26,

78; as whole, 234. *See also* Prime numbers

Numerators, 143

O

Objects, 230; in classroom, 104, 105, 119

Observations, 99, 101

Octagons, 52, 53

OECD. *See* Organisation for Economic Co-operation and Development

Operations, 226; of division, 234; flexibility and, 203–224; order of, 207, 214, 217; students choice of, 204, 208

Order, 222, 237; numbers in, 11; operations in, 207, 214, 217; symbols for, 150–156; values in, 33

Organisation for Economic Co-operation and Development (OECD), 4

Organization: of information, 221; recording as, 6, 50; for students, 93, 161, 208, 223

P

Painting Pieces activity, 145–156; agenda for, 145; discussion for, 145, 148; exploration of, 145, 148; extension of, 145, 148–149; launch of, 145, 147

Paintings: *Composition II* as, 154, 155; *Double Concentric Scramble* as, 147, 152, 153; *Red, Yellow, Blue* as, 150, 151

Paper: Centimeter Dot Paper as, 246; folding of, 19–21; Isometric Dot Paper as, 247; as materials, 18, 19–21, 121, 133, 161; 1/4" Dot Paper as, 249; 1/4" Grid Paper as, 250

Parabola, 178

Parentheses, 188

Parents, 12

Partnerships, 34, 91, 189, 207

Pattern Carnival activity, 83–87; agenda for, 83; creativity for, 83, 85–86; discussion for, 83, 86–87; launch of, 83, 85; play as, 83, 86

Patterns, 50; algebraic thinking and, 78; blocks as, 56, 59, 93; carnival of, 83–87; color-coding and, 28; discussion on, 30, 77, 86; equal groups as, 31, 41; evidence of, 54; Fibonacci as, 72, 73, 74–82, 83, 85, 87; making and naming, 71–95; models and, 199, 200; numbers as, 23–48; observations of, 198; relationships between, 102; students seeking out, 71, 76, 167, 168

Pencils: as materials, 219; price of, 222–223

Perplexing Measures activity, 118–123; agenda for, 118–119; discussion of, 119, 122; exploration as, 118, 121; extension of, 119, 122; launch of, 118, 120–121

Photos, 211; birds in, 210, 211; as materials, 205; students use of, 207, 208; wildebeests in, 212

PISA. *See* International Student Assessment

Pixeled Fractions activity, 132–141; agenda for, 132–133; discussion of, 133, 134; exploration of, 132, 134; extension of, 133, 134; launch of, 132, 134

Planes, 52, 106; tiling of, 60–61, 63

Play: carnival as, 83, 86; Color-Coding Fractions activity as, 157, 160; Decimals on a Line activity as, 234, 236; extension of, 217; ideas and, 13; Measure Up activity as, 104, 107; Pattern Carnival activity as, 83, 86; with rep-tiles, 58; Tangram Designs activity as, 124, 126–127; Those Crazy Rep-Tiles activity as, 56, 58; What Could It Be activity as, 33, 34

Play activities, 24, 50, 72, 98, 116, 204